MANAGING RICHES TOWARDS ETERNITY

DR. MIKE DUFFY

MANAGING RICHES TOWARDS ETERNITY

Words of Wisdom for the Wealthy

ISBN 979-8-9894314-5-8 (hardback)
ISBN 979-8-9894314-4-1 (paperback)
ISBN 979-8-9894314-6-5 (ebook)

All Scripture is taken from the NEW KING JAMES VERSION.

Editing by Melanie Engle, Eagle Eye Editing
Cover design and typesetting by Jenneth Dyck

Table of Contents

CHAPTER 1

WORDS OF WISDOM
FOR THE WEALTHY

I HOPE YOU FIND THIS LITTLE BOOK TO be of great benefit and blessing to your life, as it is intended to be just that. I am confident that those who invest their precious time to read it will gain a fuller understanding and appreciation for the life they are now living.

The things I will be sharing in this book are things I came to learn both through personal experience and extensive study. Considering my life's journey today, I would say that it has been a good life; however, I would also say it has been anything but normal! It would be easy to dwell on some negative times and events, but I prefer to acknowledge those, learn from them, and move ahead. This philosophy has brought me much joy and pleasure. As a means of encouragement to the reader, and to balance the content, I will share a little bit about my life as I begin this book.

I was raised in the home of an alcoholic. My parents'

marriage ended when I was in elementary school. Both of my brothers concur that we were not well parented; for the most part, we were left to find our own way alone. Much of what I learned early in life was through example and experience. There was very little instruction about the issues of life, and there were plenty of bad examples for us to learn from. The experiences, well, they have left some scars!

Our family struggled financially. Dad's addiction to booze kept the family coffers empty. As a result, our family rarely had "extra" anything, and often went without some of the basics for living. After my parents' divorce, my mother, two brothers, and I lived in a two-room cottage on main street in a little farming community in northern Illinois. We had one double bed and a couch. The first three of us home would get the bed, the other, the couch. It was like this throughout my junior-high and high school years. It was awkward!

Mom worked as a waitress, typically working every day of the week, and on some days a double-shift. While she would get a nominal paycheck regularly, most of her income was in the form of tips. At the end of her work day, she brought home a pouch of change and would have a couple dollar bills tucked into the cellophane lining of her package of Viceroy cigarettes.

Often, we boys were left to fend for ourselves. We would scrounge for whatever food we could find in the house. Quite often a meal would be some boiled macaroni with butter stirred into it. That was it! A one-course meal. I remember mom cooking some for us, but that was often limited to something like cream-of-chicken soup poured over toast.

I remember well that during the winters, frost would form

on one of the bedroom walls. It would be easy to conclude that there was little to no insulation in the walls. If we ran out of fuel-oil for the space heater, we would turn on the kitchen oven and open the door in order to heat the house. To do so, we had to leave the oven door down, and that consumed all the floor space in the kitchen! The point is, we were cramped into this little cabin. Hanging out at home was not appealing!

Somehow I developed a mind-set that money could be the avenue out of our pitiful existence. And so, instead of enjoying athletics or other extra-curricular activities in school, I got a full-time job while I was in seventh grade. I worked for an old man, George Buhl, in his little makeshift factory attached to his country home, making Stuff-a-Chick, a prepackaged stuffing for cooking with turkey or chicken.

I also had a paper route where I delivered the Rockford Morning Star to houses in the community early in the morning. I learned a little bit about selling, accounting, and the value of "tips" in that little venture! As insignificant as it may sound to do a job like that, I see now how it played an important role in my growth. Each summer, I worked a short season detasseling corn too. The money was quite good for those few weeks of work. I am sure now, as I look back on those days, that I was operating in "survival mode." I did what I thought was necessary to take care of myself and my little brother.

My early marriage and business career were spent trying to figure life out, operating with a "survival of the fittest" mindset and believing money would be the pathway to all the good things in life. While there were plenty of rough patches, the plan seemed to be working out.

My wife and I were raising three children and my career was moving in a good direction, and I was realizing some prosperity. What I was really learning was that money could be a great servant, but it could also be a terrible taskmaster. Doing the necessary often means you are not doing the desirable! The more money you make, the more opportunities you seem to have. And with those opportunities comes the pressure of responsibility.

When I was thirty-one years old I was introduced to the Gospel of Jesus Christ and, knowing my sinful self, I recognized the need for Him as my Savior. And so, on a Monday evening in January of 1980 I received Christ into my life.

With my soul and spirit now alive in Christ, I developed an insatiable appetite for spiritual food. I began to study the Bible in earnest. I was amazed at what I was learning and, by the grace of God, the Word of God was changing me. My goals and priorities were all challenged and changed. My own wisdom was challenged regularly by the wisdom of God. Much to my surprise, I soon discovered that I did not have all the answers to life. I also found out that I did not even know many of the real questions of life! The more I learned, the more I understood how much I did not know.

In the spring of 1983, I sensed the call of God on my life for full-time vocational ministry. I spent two years at Maranatha Baptist University studying and training, then entered full-time itinerant ministry as an evangelist. My family and I spent many years on the road preaching, teaching, and counseling in churches, colleges, universities, Christian camps, and Christian schools. Normally, we would spend a week at a church ministering every day and night, Sunday through Friday. On Saturday we would travel to the next church on our schedule. We would typically have 45 to 50 weeks of meetings a year. I have had the joy and privilege to preach in more than a thousand ministries across the nation and in some foreign countries.

One of my precious memories from those many years on the road with my family was this: quite often my youngest child, Kelly, would ask, "Dad, are you going to preach on the love of money tonight?" She asked that because she had been an eyewitness of my transformation from being a wealth pursuer to a minister of truth. She recognized the positive change in my life and in our family and attributed some of that change to my mindset about riches. I was not against being wealthy, it just was not the priority it once had been in my life. Other things mattered more! Kelly saw this as a positive thing for her, for me, and for our family. She was right!

The Bible teaches us that, as believers, we will one day stand at the Judgment Seat of Christ. The Apostle Paul wrote to the believers in Rome: *"But why do you judge your brother? Or why do you show contempt for your brother? For we shall all stand before the judgment seat of Christ* (Romans 14:10)." As a child of God, we will not be judged for our sin at this judgment. Remember, our sin was nailed to the cross and we bear it no more! However, this judgment will be especially important to each of us who is saved. "For what, then, will we be judged?" one might ask.

In my study of the Scriptures, I have seen two primary issues for which each of us who are redeemed believers in Jesus Christ will be called into account at the Judgment Seat of Christ: our stewardship and our service. We will either be rewarded for doing a good job, or we will suffer loss, according to the Apostle Paul's first letter to the Corinthian church. He wrote the following:

> *For we are God's fellow workers; you are God's field, you are God's building. According to the grace of God which was given to me, as a wise master builder I have laid the foundation, and another builds on it.* <u>*But let each one take heed how he builds on it.*</u> *For no other foundation can anyone lay than that which is laid, which is Jesus Christ. Now if anyone builds on this foundation with gold, silver, precious stones, wood, hay, straw, each one's work will become clear; for the Day will declare it, because it will be revealed by fire;* <u>*and the fire will test each one's work, of what sort it is. If anyone's work which he has built on it endures, he will receive a reward. If anyone's work is burned, he will suffer loss;*</u> *but he himself will be saved, yet so as through fire.*
> (1 Corinthians 3:9-15)

Although it may not always be at the forefront of our minds, the reality is that, as believers and followers of Jesus Christ, we are investing in the rest of our lives preparing for this big day. On that day, we will stand alone before the Lord, our works will be made manifest, and the judgment fires of testing will be applied to them to see what they were made of. Only those works that were profitable according to God's criteria will survive, and the criteria seems to be virtuous works with the right motive. This judgment separates what was of temporal value in our lives from what was of eternal value. Only the eternal will be meaningful and rewarded.

So, let us take some time to learn about managing the riches or wealth that God has entrusted to our care. May God bless your journey through this life and may you one day hear from the lips of Jesus Christ, "Well done, thou good and faithful servant."

CHAPTER 2

SOME FOUNDATIONAL TRUTH

In this chapter we will look at some foundational truth that will both establish the authority for these teachings and bring confidence and encouragement to you to implement the principles.

GOD'S UNCHANGING WORD

This first foundational truth is found in Psalm 119:89 where the Bible states: "*Forever, O LORD, Your word is settled in heaven.*" This is such a key place to begin. As one invests their time and energy to read, study, and meditate on God's Word to learn about their role and responsibility as a steward, and then begin to apply it to their own life's context, they can do so with the greatest assurance that halfway through the game of life, the truth will not change. God's Word is settled! God does not and will not change His thinking or His mind about that. He said, *"For I am the LORD, I do not change* (Malachi 3:6a)."

It matters not in what part of the world you may live, what your economic status might be, or what your family or culture has historically taught you; God's Word will not change. What someone believes does not change the truth.

The appropriate thing to do when we are confronted with Bible truth is to let God's Word change us! After all, for the believer, this is what sanctification is all about—being conformed to the image of Christ. Simply put, we are engaged in a lifelong process of change! God uses His Word to accomplish that change. It shows us what is wrong, how to fix that which needs fixing, and it tells us how to keep things working properly.

GOD MADE EVERYTHING

A second foundational truth to consider is this: God is the Creator of everything. He is *the* Maker, and He is *our* Maker. *"In the beginning God created the heavens and the earth* (Genesis 1:1)." This same chapter also tells us how God created it: *"Then God said, "Let there be light"; and there was light. And God saw the light, that it was good; and God divided the light from the darkness* (Genesis 1:3-4)." He "said" it. He spoke the worlds into existence. Look at the rest of chapter one and you will see over and over God speaking creation into being (verses 6, 9, 11, 14, 20, 24, and 26).

I would be remiss not to acknowledge there are many who do not believe this first verse of the Bible. There are people of all ages who try to ignore this truth for fear of becoming accountable to God. As a result of their unbelief, they produce their own theories, such as the big bang theory, the theory of evolution, spontaneous generation, cosmogenesis, and others. While we are all free to believe whatever we choose to believe, what one believes does not change God's truth! God is the Creator, and all of mankind is accountable to God.

I have often wondered, "If a person will not believe the first verse of the Bible, will they believe any of it? Why would you believe some of it and not other parts of the Bible? Who determines in one's mind which parts to believe and which parts to reject? Would that not be akin to playing the role of God in your own life?" When it comes right down to it, the foolishness and audacity to play that role is stunning! Why would one have such a high opinion of themselves that they would even begin to consider challenging the ways of God?

If one fears becoming accountable to God, well, the truth is that they are already accountable to Him. We are all accountable to God; whether we understand or believe this, we are accountable to Him. It would be accurate to say, "Time will tell." But if you take him at his Word too late, it will be eternally too late! Unbelief is what sends people to Hell. This is why our search for truth should be a diligent search.

The Apostle Paul, writing to the church in Colossae and speaking of Jesus Christ, declared that "*For by Him all things were created that are in heaven and that are on earth, visible and invisible, whether thrones or dominions or principalities or powers. All things were created through Him and for Him. And He is before all things, and in Him all things consist,* (to be held together) (Colossians 1:16-17)." God is the Creator and Sustainer of all things. All things were created by Him, and they were created for Him—that is, for His pleasure. He existed before any of the creation, and He continues to hold it all together today. He is the all-powerful, all-knowing, eternal, self-existent One. He is God.

IT ALL BELONGS TO GOD

Everything belongs to God! He is the Creator of everything. He owns it! As David prays to God when he is praying over the offerings the people had given to build the temple, David makes this incredible statement. He says, *"But who am I, and who are my people, that we should be able to offer so willingly as this? For all things come from You, and of Your own we have given You* (1 Chronicles 29:14)." The people were giving their offering to praise and honor God by simply giving back to God that which He had entrusted to them to manage. It was all His in the first place. Their gifts to Him were from Him! What a mind bender!

As a father, I can relate to their offering in this way: it is like a parent giving some money to their child so the child can buy a gift for the parent. I remember my parents doing this when I was a child. Back then, I did not really think about where I got the money to purchase the gift, I was just happy to give the present. I felt like I was the one giving! Later in life my wife and I did the same thing with our children. They gave to us like they were giving us something of theirs.

King David, as the Psalmist, wrote: *"The earth is the LORD's, and all its fullness, the world and those who dwell therein* (Psalm 24:1)." He also wrote, *"The heavens are Yours, the earth also is Yours; The world and all its fullness, You have founded them* (Psalm 89:11)." The prophet Haggai wrote, *"'The silver is Mine, and the gold is Mine,' says the LORD of hosts* (Haggai 2:8)." We could go on and on as this truth is consistently stated throughout the Bible. It all belongs to God—everything!

Since everything belongs to God, we can understand that man is not the owner (or even the co-owner), rather he is a steward. By having possessions, he is tasked with managing a portion of the household of God. This includes things that are quite significant to us, such as time, talents (giftedness), and treasure.

As a steward, man is a trustee! God trusts him to execute God's will with God's stuff. How the man does his job is evaluated by God, and man will be commended (rewarded) accordingly by God at the Judgment Seat of Christ. This is God's accountability.

THERE IS A DIFFERENCE BETWEEN STEWARDSHIP AND OWNERSHIP

One might ask, "What is the difference between an owner and a steward?" The answer is simple: "Who gets to set the agenda?" The owner sets the agenda! The steward's role is to manage the tasks that will fulfill the owner's agenda. Our responsibility then, is to do the will of the owner—God. It is not to pursue our own aspirations and desires. We do this by seeking God's will and then doing it.

For more on this issue, you may want to study James 4:13-16, where one learns that leaving God's will out of their discernment and decision making is an evil practice. Here is what the passage says:

> *Come now, you who say, "Today or tomorrow we will go to such and such a city, spend a year there, buy and sell, and make a profit;" whereas you do not know what will happen tomorrow. For what is your life? It is even a vapor that appears for a little time and then vanishes away. Instead you ought to say, "If the Lord wills, we shall live and do this or that." But now you boast in your arrogance. All such boasting is evil.* (James 4:13-16)

It is the Lord Who holds tomorrow! He knows what is coming for us. It is He Who is the giver and taker of life. Our time comes and goes quickly; seeking and doing the will of God should be our priority. To presume upon God, or to exalt our own will above His, is arrogant. It is pride and it is evil. That is what James is teaching us!

In the parable of the talents in Matthew 25, Jesus commended two of the servants for increasing that which the master had entrusted to them through good management. When the time for accounting came for each of these stewards, God's Word tells us, "*His lord said to him, 'Well done, good and faithful servant; you were faithful over a few things, I will make you ruler over many things. Enter into the joy of your lord'* (Matthew 25:21)." It should be the desire of every believer to receive this same commendation as they stand face-to-face before the Lord at the Judgment Seat of Christ and give account of their stewardship.

It seems as though one problem many have today is that they do not really know "why" they possess all the treasure or wealth that they have. Having more than what they need creates the pressure to understand why they possess it and what they should do with it. Often they have no sense of responsibility for the proper use of their wealth, and neither, then, do they have any sense of accountability! The treasure is considered just "extra," and they can do whatever they feel like doing with it. The ways of the world have influenced this kind of thinking. Some just feel guilty because they possess more than others they know. And so, through misunderstanding or ignorance, life and opportunity just go on. Incredible opportunities for biblical stewardship just pass them by, drifting into the future, going unmet and unaddressed, without any recognition from the steward.

God has a plan for what He has entrusted to us; our ignorance is not God's fault. He has given us many principles in His Word for managing His stuff and telling us about our responsibilities. That includes both our personal needs and the resources we possess that are beyond our own needs. There is a day of accountability coming, and we must not ignore that! It would be a healthy exercise to ask yourself, "How prepared am I to answer to God for my activity with the wealth I am currently holding by the grace of God?"

A Picture of Gracious Generosity

In writing his second letter to the Church at Corinth, the Apostle Paul describes what gracious generosity looks like. From this description, we can learn some important truths that will help

21

us exercise our stewardship of the riches God entrusts to our care. Paul writes the following:

> *Moreover, brethren, we make known to you the grace of God bestowed on the churches of Macedonia: that in a great trial of affliction the abundance of their joy and their deep poverty abounded in the riches of their liberality. For I bear witness that according to their ability, yes, and beyond their ability, they were freely willing, imploring us with much urgency that we would receive the gift and the fellowship of the ministering to the saints. And not only as we had hoped, but they first gave themselves to the Lord, and then to us by the will of God. So we urged Titus, that as he had begun, so he would also complete this grace in you as well. But as you abound in everything—in faith, in speech, in knowledge, in all diligence, and in your love for us—see that you abound in this grace also.*
> (2 Corinthians 8:1-7)

The first thing we can learn from Paul's instruction is that we need to recognize that our ability to be generous is only because of the grace—or enablement—of God. Paul wanted the Corinthian believers to understand that God had "bestowed" that grace on the churches of Macedonia (Berea, Philippi, and Thessalonica). It was this grace that was the power behind their generous and sacrificial giving. It is vital that we recognize this grace for our lives too!

The next lesson has to do with the circumstances in which these generous givers found themselves. They themselves were deep in a difficult trial of life, and yet their joy in the Lord was abundant. Their joy was not determined by life's circumstances, but rather it was determined by their relationship with the Lord. They could not control the circumstances of life, but they could control themselves in their walk with God. Even though their circumstances included "deep poverty," they could be liberal in their giving. And not just liberal, but rich!

Next, in verse three, we see that they were able to give "beyond their power." This giving was not coerced, they were giving willingly. They wanted to give generously. Does that not speak of unselfishness? A faithful walk with God will result in overcoming our selfish tendencies and priorities.

This leads us to the next important point, found in verse five. Do not miss this sequence. They first surrendered their will to the Lord. In other words, they cleared the slate of their own ideas and desires. It would be like handing the Lord your own "to do" list that was blank, and then asking Him to fill in the blanks according to His desire and ideas.

After making this surrender, they were then ready to listen to what the Lord would have them to do. He got to set the agenda or fill out the "to do" list. Then, once they received the list from the Lord, they did it! They gave by the will of God. God enabled and instructed them regarding their generous giving, and so they gave richly and willingly.

I thought it would be worth including the following thought from my study of this portion of Scripture. Strong's Concordance pointed out that the Greek verb "didōmi" in this context ("they first gave"), meant "to one demanding of me something, I give myself up as it were; an hyperbole for disregarding entirely my private interests, I give as much as ever I can: II Corinthians

8:5."[1] This really helped me capture the spirit of what Paul was saying to the Corinthian believers.

Paul was using the example of the churches of Macedonia as an example for the church at Corinth. He wanted Pastor Titus to continue teaching these Christians about gracious giving. He was to encourage the congregation by pointing out how well they were doing in other graces of the Christian life, then exhort them to exercise this grace also—the grace of generous giving.

I remember a time when I was with a ministry leader, a college president, and we were approaching the home of a prospective donor. I had arranged the meeting. I shared some thoughts with him from this same passage. One could certainly see the concept of "faith promise" or "matching gift" principles at work. The Corinthian church had made a commitment to give a year earlier. Paul used that commitment to challenge other churches about giving to the same need, or cause, which was relief for the Jerusalem Christians who were in great distress. Now Paul was encouraging the Corinthians to follow through with their pledge. The college president used the thoughts as he was discussing with this wealthy man the possibility of partnering with their ministry.

THE BIGGER BARNS TRAP

Living in a world of opportunity and prospering in a free nation as an American, one is especially prone to this temptation and trap. There is much that appeals to us, and, for many, the resources to obtain them makes it all possible. It is not wrong to gather riches or enjoy some of the pleasures of this world that God wants us to enjoy. The main point of the lesson Jesus teaches in a parable in the Gospel of Luke which we are about to consider is this: "*So is he that lays up treasure for himself and is not rich toward God.*" Jesus was addressing the issue of covetousness. The lesson is from the parable in Luke 12:13-21. It reads as follows:

> *Then one from the crowd said to Him, "Teacher, tell my brother to divide the inheritance with me." But He said to him, "Man, who made Me a judge or an arbitrator over you?" And He said to them, "Take heed and beware of covetousness, for one's life does not consist in the abundance of the things he possesses."*
> *Then He spoke a parable to them, saying: "The ground of a certain rich man yielded plentifully. And he thought within himself, saying, 'What shall I do, since I have no room to store my crops?' So he said, 'I will do this: I will pull down my barns and build greater, and there I will store all my crops and my goods. And I will say to my soul, "Soul, you have many goods laid up for many years; take your ease; eat, drink, and be merry." But God said to him, 'Fool! This night your soul will be required of you; then whose will those things be which you have provided?' So is he who lays up treasure for himself, and is not rich toward God."* (Luke 12:13-21)

Here is the context of the passage we are looking at. The Lord was speaking to His disciples, and a large crowd (an innumerable multitude) was gathered there listening. As he spoke, Jesus warned His disciples to beware of the leaven of the Pharisees, which was hypocrisy—deceit; acting one way and really being another. The point Jesus was making was that He knew their hearts. He knew everything about them, and so they should not try to deceive Him. It was impossible to do so. Judgment day would come, and the truth would be revealed. Therefore, he exhorted the crowd to fear God, not man. It was God Who knew the most intricate details of their lives, and He was the one with authority and power to forgive sins. They were ultimately accountable to Him.

In the midst of His teaching, a man stepped forward out of the crowd and made an interesting request: "*Teacher, tell my brother to divide the inheritance with me.*" Just a side note here, did you notice the issue? A dispute over an inheritance. Riches hold incredible potential for disputes, especially when they are left to another in a will or a trust! That alone would be a good lesson for us to learn. We will reserve that for another book, however, it has significant relevance to what we are considering. Do you possess riches that are to be used now, or are they to be passed to the next generation? You will certainly want to determine the answer to that question. Jesus rebuked the man by saying: "*Man, who made Me a judge or an arbitrator over you?*" Remember, the Lord didn't just hear the question, He knew the man's heart! He knew WHY he asked the question.

Jesus then turned back to the crowd and warns His disciples: "*And He said to them, "Take heed and beware of covetousness, for one's life does not consist in the abundance of the things he possesses.*" It was obvious that this was a big issue with the man that asked the Lord to settle the dispute with his brother, and so, by the analogy the Lord used (*of what man's life consisted*), He warned all of these people about an issue that was relative to every one of them— covetousness! Our life is about much more than things or stuff!

Then Jesus illustrates the truth with a parable. In this

earthly story which has a heavenly meaning, Jesus uses thirteen possessive pronouns. Quoting the rich man, He uses the word "I" six times, highlighting the man's selfish spirit. Let's look at some important parts of the text from which we can learn some important lessons for life!

The first lesson is the obvious lesson: Beware of covetousness! Watch out, be on guard, and recognize its presence and its destructive power. Covetousness is greediness or desiring to hold more. It is having a self-centered hunger for something you do not possess. For anyone possessing riches, the frequency of temptations toward covetousness are like the waves of the sea splashing on the shore. They keep coming at us. Relentlessly, they keep coming and coming!

The Apostle Paul instructed Pastor Timothy to warn his church members about covetousness when he wrote the following:

> But those who desire to be rich fall into temptation and a snare, and into many foolish and harmful lusts which drown men in destruction and perdition. For the love of money is a root of all kinds of evil, for which some have strayed from the faith in their greediness, and pierced themselves through with many sorrows. (1 Timothy 6:9-10)

This is the passage my daughter kept referring to when asking me if I was preaching about the love of money.

Covetousness breaks the tenth commandment—not to covet thy neighbor's house. Does it make you wonder if the neighbor that Moses refers to had a bigger or better house? Or maybe the location was better? Covetousness comes out of the heart. Mark wrote in his Gospel:

> *And He said, "What comes out of a man, that defiles a man. For from within, out of the heart of men, proceed evil thoughts, adulteries, fornications, murders, thefts, covetousness, wickedness, deceit, lewdness, an evil eye, blasphemy, pride, foolishness. All these evil things come from within and defile a man."* (Mark 7:20-23)

We can learn from Jesus' teaching, recorded by Mark, that a covetous heart will be allured with the appealing offers of fulfillment and happiness. Unfortunately, the one offering these opportunities cannot deliver on the offer! How deceitful! Covetousness is a greed that makes us drunk with desire to the point of distorting our thinking and capturing our devotion. It is evil.

How common is the understanding of the covetous nature of the human heart? Well, consider the appeal of some of the TV game shows that have been popular through the years. They include shows like *Let's Make a Deal*, *Greed*, *Deal or No Deal*, and the list could go on. What do they have in common? In their pursuit for more, many times on these shows, contestants behave as though they were in a drunken stupor with their foolish and greedy choices! Covetousness is the passion that drives the gambler to eventual destruction and loss. So appealing is the opportunity and excitement that it becomes an addiction for many. They lose control of their ability to stop or say no. The nature of covetousness seems to be *"Enough is never enough!"*

We might say the next lesson is to beware of foolishness.

This man was the recipient of an abundant blessing—a great crop. The harvest he had was a greater blessing than he had ever experienced, as is evidenced by his inability to contain it in his existing barns. He had never possessed more in his lifetime! Foolishly, he gave no consideration as to whom that blessing came from. Think for a moment about everything you have. Where did it come from? It seems that people rarely ask themselves this question. And this, perhaps, is where they begin to go astray.

Everything that we possess, God has entrusted to our care! Consider these Bible truths: "*Every good gift and every perfect gift is from above, and comes down from the Father of lights, with whom there is no variation or shadow of turning* (James 1:17)." And Moses wrote, "*And you shall remember the LORD your God, for it is He who gives you power to get wealth* (Deuteronomy 8:18a)."

Because the farmer's thought process did not consider the source, he did not know what to do with the blessing. Instead, he asked another question. "What shall I do? I don't have room to store all this." This is the problem many have today. They do not really know why they have all that they have. His thoughts immediately went to "storing the stuff." With no purpose, there is no sense of responsibility, and so, no sense of accountability! That is not good!

While it was foolish not to consider where the blessing came from or why he possessed it, the foolishness is compounded by what he does next. He goes to himself for counsel!

How arrogant is this! "*He thought within himself.*" Like many today, he was self-reliant and self-governed! In his pride, he believed that he knew best! In Jeremiah 10:23 the prophet offers

29

some sobering truth we all need to understand. He wrote, "*O LORD, I know the way of man is not in himself; It is not in man who walks to direct his own steps.*"

Once a person grasps the truth of Jeremiah's statement and they truly believe this, they will more readily seek counsel from God and His Word. They will seek godly counsel from wise men who know the Word. The Bible teaches us that there is wisdom in a multitude of counselors.

A counselor's role is not to make your decisions for you; rather, it is to guide you with truth to seek and fulfill God's will with what He has entrusted to your care.

The farmer's foolish thoughts now lead to foolish planning. He produced a plan all right! "*This will I do.*" Here is his plan in a nutshell: "I will just store the blessing away for me!" Clean the closet, basement, attic, and garage! Make room to store more! If that is not enough, I will rent a storage unit! He would tear down his existing storage barns and build larger barns that could hold the entirety of this bumper crop. Does that not sound foolish too? Why tear down his existing barn? Why not build an additional barn?

We do not have to read his mind to see what motivated his foolish thinking and planning. He tells us with this next statement: "*And I will say to my soul, Soul, you have many goods laid up for many years; take your ease; eat, drink, and be merry.*" He was saying to himself, "*I will comfort myself with the abundance.*" Right there we see his source of confidence—his purpose in the provision and the false hope for a coming peace. His faith and confidence were in his own abundance! And his earthly goal was all about himself. How sad!

While one might be tempted to say, "This sounds good to me!" ask yourself, as a child of God, "Does this sound to you like a battlefield strategy?" Oh, my fellow Christian, have you lost sight of the fact that we are living on a battlefield and not a playground? The spiritual warfare is raging all around us. It has been raging since the Garden of Eden. The Master is engaged in the battle, and He wants to direct us to do our part in winning the war. This man was oblivious to this truth!

I will admit that I have a difficult time believing he understood God and his Word. By reading the Bible cover to cover, studying it, and meditating on the truths I learn from it, it is hard to escape the fact that God has a plan for mankind and that it includes involving His people to execute the plan.

This man's plan was flawed! He had a misunderstanding of the purpose of the blessing. He thought the storage of these things would last a long time and provide comfort, provision, satisfaction, and happiness FOR HIM; all self-centered thoughts and ideas! His plan does not indicate that he thought of the responsibilities, challenges, difficulties, and dangers it may bring, nor did he look for the opportunities it provided. He was drunk with covetousness. His plan was short sighted. He had no strategy beyond storage! Why, one might ask? Because building wealth for himself was his cause, it was the end in and of itself, not a means to a greater end!

He had apparently missed God's bigger purpose for why he was being blessed with the abundant crop. With no relationship with the Lord, it is easy to miss this purpose. Without a long-range plan, how would he know when he had grown beyond provision to surplus? How much would be enough? How much we think is enough for provision speaks to the lifestyle choices we make. What will my standard of living be? What investments will I make in the kingdom of God? Each of us has to make these choices. Have you made your choices wisely? Biblically?

His plan was foolish. In verse twenty we see more evidence for that conclusion. We learn that he had no consideration neither for the length of life, nor for the one Who is the giver and taker of life. This is important for us to know so that we can maintain a biblical perspective of possessions. Riches and wealth are temporal, and we will not be taking them with us to heaven. Consider Paul's statement to Timothy: "*For we brought nothing into this world, and it is certain we can carry nothing out* (1 Timothy 6:7)." There is an old saying that I have heard many times—"You never see a hearse pulling a U-Haul trailer!"

Job helps us put a proper perspective on the issue, too. "*And he said: 'Naked I came from my mother's womb, and naked shall I return there. The LORD gave, and the LORD has taken away; Blessed be the name of the LORD'* (Job 1:21)."

All of these foundational truths will help us as we look at the issue at hand, managing our riches towards eternity.

CHAPTER 3

WHY YOUR PASTOR NEEDS TO LEARN AND TEACH BIBLICAL FINANCIAL STEWARDSHIP

GOD HAS PLACED EACH OF US WHO ARE born again into the church that Jesus is building. It is there that we can grow in the grace and knowledge of the Lord Jesus. He has called some to be pastors and teachers, and some He has gifted as evangelists to help us in our Christian growth. This growth includes the exercise of our service and stewardship. These servants of God watch for our souls. One of the reasons they watch for us is so that our reward is full and we lose none of it (see 1 Corinthians 3:14-15).

The steward's requirement is faithfulness to the Lord. This means being faithful in both service and stewardship, not simply in church service attendance. Growing in grace is about relationship, while attending church services has more to do with religion.

In this chapter, I have an important point to make, and it is this: your pastor has a *responsibility* to minister to you in matters regarding stewardship, and that includes financial stewardship. He is to help you prepare for your accountability to the Lord in this matter. It will be helpful to you to understand the pastor's role as you sit under his teaching, preaching, and counseling. Your pastor will help you grow in the grace and knowledge of the Lord Jesus.

One of the most difficult areas of ministry for a preacher is preaching and teaching about financial matters; in short, MONEY! I know that because I am a preacher; I have ministered to and alongside several hundred preachers in my lifetime. Ask any pastor you know how difficult it is for him to address this issue. Even the most educated and seasoned pastors experience some level of anxiety when addressing financial issues. There are very few who would tell you it is easy for them. The first thing you will notice, even before you hear him say anything in response to the question, is how uncomfortable he becomes when asked the question. Why is that? Why does addressing this issue cause the preacher so much distress?

While there may be many reasons, it is my experience that preachers do not like to address financial issues because they do not want folks to perceive that all they are interested in is extracting money from the church members to support their ministries. There exists a real stigma that this is so. Does "fleecing the flock" ring a bell? Have you watched what goes on when a preacher gets a media outlet? It seems like much of the airtime is spent trying to extract money from the viewers. They are selling all kinds of merchandise, claiming they contain spiritual power. You often hear them make the "crisis appeal of the day" to stir the emotional giving from vulnerable people.

To avoid the perception that the pastor is "money hungry," or that all he ever speaks about is money, the pastor simply avoids the topic altogether. After all, he reasons, there is a lot more in the Bible to speak about that needs urgent attention!

While there certainly are other important issues, there is much written about the responsibility and exercise of stewardship. Someone once concluded that there is more written in the Bible about money and its management than there is about heaven, hell, and love combined. I do not know if that is the case, but the point is made. There is much written in Scripture that the believer needs to learn about stewardship. He needs to learn it because he is called to be a steward, and he will one day give account for his stewardship.

It may also be the pastor's inadequacy in his own personal stewardship that causes him to avoid the subject. Getting deep into a conversation with another person about financial matters, and particularly financial problems, may result in exposing his own shortcomings. This is a constant pressure for a pastor. This kind of pressure is not just about money, but many other issues as well. The pastor is certainly not an expert in everything; however, he is to be skilled in ministering God's Word.

It may also be that, because they are struggling in a particular area of life, the devil makes them think that they should not be addressing these issues in anyone else's life. While a pastor's experience and example may be lacking, the truth is always appropriate for everyone. It is the truth of God, applied by the Holy Spirit of God, which brings about life-changing conviction. The pastor is simply the messenger of God to deliver His truth. If a pastor does feel inadequate, or is doing a poor job in some area, then he should do something about it! He should learn it so he can teach it better, and more confidently.

To add to this last point with a little personal transparency—as a minister of the Gospel, the more I learn of Scripture, the more inadequate I feel. Does that mean I should no longer teach or preach the Bible? Heavens, no! It reveals that I am growing, and I have a lot more growing to do. And to further add to the discussion, how adequate do you think Peter thought he was as he preached on the day of Pentecost after his colossal failure on the day they crucified the Lord? The power is in the author and the message, not the messenger. I must admit, sometimes we as preachers just get in the way of what God is trying to do.

So, what ends up happening when a pastor is reluctant to teach biblical financial stewardship? The people in the church remain relatively untaught in their biblical responsibility, and thus are prone to, on one hand, make a financial mess out of their life, and on the other hand, fail to get a "full reward" at the judgment seat of Christ. Many believe the subject of money is "taboo" when it comes to ministry. I would say just the opposite. It is very important to learn what God says about managing financial affairs. To not do so is setting up the flock (for which he has oversight) for trouble now and experiencing loss at the Judgment Seat! Everyone faces money issues, and Paul warned Timothy in his letter that the love of money was "the root of all evil."

Having preached in several hundred churches and spending time with the pastors of those churches, I learned that pastors are very uncomfortable about financial issues, but they are often confronted with them. I also witnessed many occasions where financial misconduct or mismanagement ended the ministry of a pastor. As sad as that is, the harsh reality is that it is all too common.

As one studies the Scriptures, they begin to realize there is a real sense that the primary role of a pastor is to prepare those in his congregation for their "big day." That big day is when they stand before the Lord Jesus at the Judgment Seat of Christ, also known as the BEMA seat. It is not managing the everyday affairs of each member, and it is not making all the financial decisions for the church members. It is making disciples who are answerable to the Lord. Honestly, I have met many pastors who operate as though they had authority over another's financial affairs. I have also met church members who ascribe to the same philosophy. Neither of these are found in the Scriptures.

As the Apostle Paul writes his letters to Timothy, Timothy is a pastor. He has the responsibility before God, and, as the Apostle Peter put it, to "*Shepherd the flock of God which is among you, serving as overseers, not by compulsion but willingly, not for dishonest gain but eagerly* (1 Peter 5:2)." Paul is writing to strengthen Timothy's ministry to his people, and he tells him "*These things I write to you, though I hope to come to you shortly; but if I am delayed, I write so that you may know how you ought to conduct yourself in the house of God, which is the church of the living God, the pillar and ground of the truth* (1 Timothy 3:14-15)." In plain English—Timothy, here is how to do your ministry!

With this understanding, consider what Paul instructs Timothy to do as he brings this first letter to a close. I remember well the study session when I first understood the true relevance of 1 Timothy 6:17-21. I was in awe, and at the same time I could sense a feeling of comfort, realizing that God had a plan for people to manage riches and enjoy them. It was one of those "aha!" moments in life. I can only imagine, however, that this exhortation may have raised Pastor Timothy's blood pressure a little! Paul wrote the following:

> *Command those who are rich in this present age not to be haughty, nor to trust in uncertain riches but in the living God, who gives us richly all things to enjoy. Let them do good, that they be rich in good works, ready to give, willing to share, storing up for themselves a good foundation for the time to come, that they may lay hold on eternal life.*
>
> *O Timothy! Guard what was committed to your trust, avoiding the profane and idle babblings and contradictions of what is falsely called knowledge—by professing it some have strayed concerning the faith. Grace be with you. Amen.*
> (I Timothy 6:17-21)

Notice the first word in this text; "command." The word means "give command."[2] In other words, it was Pastor Timothy's God-given responsibility to minister to folks who were rich in this world about their riches. He was to do so whether he was comfortable doing it or not! This single verse breaks an age-old myth that says, "My money is only my business." If this has been your mindset, well, hold on a minute there, partner! In the first place it is not "my" money, it's God's money! And second, your pastor has the God-given responsibility and authority to teach and preach to you about the riches you possess so you manage it properly for God's glory.

In this context, he is to address the rich person about their attitude toward riches, their activity with riches, and the accomplishment of that right attitude and appropriate activity. He also warns of misuse. We will look at each of these issues individually later in this book. By the way, earlier in chapter 6, the Apostle Paul points out that the rich are those who have more than food and raiment, or food and shelter. That means there are many in need of this teaching who do not consider themselves to be rich. They are to manage the riches they have, however much that may be.

For now, in order to strengthen our understanding and ability to manage the rich resources of God, let us ask this question, and then answer it: "Why does your pastor need to learn biblical financial stewardship and teach it regularly?"

PERSONAL BENEFIT

First of all, the pastor should learn financial stewardship for the benefit of his own life. He, too, has a personal relationship with the Lord, and thus, he is a steward of God's stuff. God requires him to be a faithful steward. Consider the following:

> Let a man so consider us, as servants of Christ and stewards of the mysteries of God. Moreover it is required in stewards that one be found faithful. But with me it is a very small thing

that I should be judged by you or by a human court. In fact, I do not even judge myself. For I know of nothing against myself, yet I am not justified by this; but He who judges me is the Lord. Therefore judge nothing before the time, until the Lord comes, who will both bring to light the hidden things of darkness and reveal the counsels of the hearts. Then each one's praise will come from God. (1 Corinthians 4:1-5)

A pastor's work is serving and pleasing the Lord, not meeting the approval of people. As an under-shepherd for the Great Shepherd, he is to be driven by truth, responsibility, and duty, not by the opinions of people. He knows the Lord will be his judge. So, he is to faithfully go about his work in the right way, and with the right motive in his heart. It is sad but true that a people pleaser is rarely a faithful truth teller! Speaking the truth in love is the pastor's task.

Providing for His Family

Like any other believer, the pastor has the responsibility to provide for his family. One chapter earlier in Paul's letter, he makes this clear to Timothy. *"But if anyone does not provide for his own, and especially for those of his household, he has denied the faith and is worse than an unbeliever* (1 Timothy 5:8)."

In my early experience at Bible college, I heard a number of teachers tell the students studying for the ministry something like, "As you go out into ministry, do not make money a point of discussion or decision," as though this piety or virtue was God's plan. It was expected for "the man of God" to sacrifice. Poverty was admired and exalted. This was terrible advice! It totally ignored a man's responsibility to provide for his own family, and possibly for his parents or in-laws. One would never tell a person going into the workforce to ignore the issue of compensation.

Meditate on this verse for a significant period of time and you will be surprised at what you can learn from it. As you do, I think you will have a fuller understanding of the following issues.

The Responsibility for Financial Stewardship Belongs to the Husband.

The husband provides for *his* own and *his* own house, and if *he* does not, *he* has denied the faith. These are masculine pronouns. The husband carries the burden of responsibility for the financial affairs of his family. This is a responsibility/accountability issue. In God's structure for the family (we could also say "in God's economy"), there is order and sequence. The man is the head of the woman, and thus the head of his family (see also 1 Corinthians 11:3, 2 Corinthians 5:9-10, and Ephesians 5:21-22). This is not meant to produce a competition or conflict between the husband and the wife. Women are equal in value but different in function. While he is the leader, she is the completer! A husband's responsibility does not prevent the woman from helping the man with the family's plan for financial matters, even executing part of their plan. She can do so, but remember, she is the completer of the man. He must carry this burden! God equipped him, not her, to carry it, and that is what Paul is pointing out here.

PROVIDING IS THE HUSBAND'S RESPONSIBILITY.

Although this sounds like we are being redundant, this next thought is focused on the word "provide" found in this verse. It means "to consider in advance, or to look out for beforehand."[3] It is the concept of proactive planning.

The husband, because of his understanding of both his stewardship and leadership responsibilities, should develop the plan for his family. When we say "develop," it is more about discovering God's will in Scripture and formulating the plan so one can make application of Bible principles to their own life context, than it is about creating a plan from their own imagination for pursuing personal dreams and fantasies. It should focus on the needs and provisions for his family. His wife should have liberty to provide opinion and input into the development of their family plan. After all, the two have become one—a single unit.

I like to look at the process this way: there is a leader (you might say "beginner"), and there is a follower, or "completer." They are both part of the same team. "Together," they should discover God's plan for their lives and then execute the plan.

THE SCOPE OF THE HUSBAND'S PLAN SHOULD EXTEND BEYOND "HIS OWN."

As you look closely at this verse and ruminate on its application, you will notice a distinction between "*his own*" and "*especially those of his own house.*" The plan is to be broad enough in scope that, in an emergency, he could care for his widowed mother or mother-in-law. So, his plan goes beyond himself, his wife, and their children. It extends to the care of their parents as they grow old and become unable to make provision for themselves.

So, as a young man looks toward the future, he considers in advance, or looks out for beforehand, the time when he and his wife might be caring for a parent. This could be an added burden of time, attention, and money when that happens. His plan then should include a saving provision that will meet the financial demand for this future event. Early planning will make the responsibility of care later much easier.

This principle is quite relevant in our day, as the life expectancy of women is greater than that of men in most countries. In most developed countries, that difference is between five and six years. So, it is highly likely that a middle-aged couple would be assuming the care for the widowed mother of either the husband or wife, or perhaps both. If the need arises, the responsibility becomes reality. A good man will begin making provision for this event early. He is the "default" plan if his father or father-in-law has failed in making adequate provision.

It was ironic that, while I was discussing this manuscript with a friend, I learned that a pastor with whom I had served (and who had built a church in a neighboring state) was now nearing eighty years old. Many pastor friends admired him. He had served that congregation for more than 40 years. And he is still the pastor! He cannot retire! He has to continue to work to get a paycheck. He did not do well with his personal responsibility to himself and his family, instead making sure that the church property was paid off and the ministry had everything it needed He and his wife have no provision for retirement, and they certainly would not be able to provide care for others because of their inability to financially support the effort.

Yes, Jesus could come at any moment, but we need to plan on being here until He comes, no matter how long that is. The principles of Scripture teach us so.

Failure to Do So Is to Reject Biblical Truth

It has been my experience that if you ask people to complete the following sentence, they will err in their answer. Here is the sentence: "But if anyone does not provide for his own, and especially for those of his household, he_____." You fill in the blank! After a moment of thought, they will usually answer, "is worse than an unbeliever (or "infidel" in the KJV)." While we do see this answer later in the verse, this phrase is not what comes next in the sentence. The sentence says that if he does not provide, "*he has denied the faith*." The faith in the sentence contains a definite article, so it is talking about "the faith" or the revealed body of truth, the Word of God. In other words, he is a Bible rejector! That is what makes him "*worse than an infidel*." He is a saved person rejecting God's truth, and in God's mind, that is worse than being an unbeliever who rejects the truth. This thought should give us some understanding of how important the issue of personal stewardship is to God. It should also provide an incentive to get our proverbial ducks in a row in this area of our lives.

And think about the faith challenge this is, which is healthy for anyone to consider. The Bible instructs us that a diligent steward's plan leads to profit. "*The plans of the diligent lead surely to plenty, but those of everyone who is hasty, surely to poverty* (Proverbs 21:5)." This is Bible truth, not the prosperity gospel. Do you believe this? Do you?

"*The plans*"[4] speaks of the fabrication, the forecast, or the plan that one discovers and determines to accomplish. They learn and assemble the principles that instruct the practice of stewardship, thus formulating a plan. As believers, we all need to plan, looking toward the future.

"*Of the diligent*" speaks of the character and effort of the steward. Be diligent in the study and preparation of a plan, and then diligently implement the plan into their life context. Solomon will offer a contrast later in the proverb.

"*Lead surely to plenty*," plenty meaning "profit." The diligent effort (sowing) results in plenty, or profit (reaping). In other words, it was worth the effort and of value to the steward. And do not overlook the word "surely." It could be translated as "only." If we truly believe that the planning of a diligent person results only in profit, why would we not do it? God's principles and promises will never fail! A biblical plan leads "surely" to profit!

In the same verse, we see a contrast as Solomon speaks of someone with a different character or effort when he says, "*But of every one who is hasty*," or those who are in a hurry, or who withdraw, or quit. This is the one who makes no diligent effort to prepare a plan. They ignore the principles and promises of God. They "do their own thing." It seems as though there is not a proactive bone in their body! He demonstrates a significant level of laziness and irresponsibility. It may also be apathy or apostasy.

The result of this person's life philosophy is sad but expected.

45

It leads to "*Only to poverty*," or "want." The lack of effort (sowing) results in poverty (reaping). Encountering people like this is all too common, and it is really sad to observe. You can find them clustered in communities in cities with large populations of people who are in the same situation, depending on handouts from others for their basic needs. You can see them panhandling on street corners or lining the streets with tent-cities. They stand in lines at soup kitchens and rescue shelters wanting only another meal, or a night of safety and rest. There is a great cost to rejecting God's truth!

So, as the pastor plans and executes his own plan, and as the Lord blesses the plan, the pastor will have confidence to minister the Word of God in this area. Like the Apostle Paul, he will be able to say, "*For I have not shunned to declare to you the whole counsel of God* (Acts 20:27)."

Personal Testimony in the Community

The pastor also has an especially important personal testimony to maintain in the community. In fact, it is one of the requirements to serve as a pastor that he is "blameless as the steward of God" (see Matthew 5:16, I Timothy 3:7, and Titus 1:7). Many pastors feel as though they live in a "glass house," and that people are always ready and willing to throw stones at it! Failing to practice sound financial stewardship is like handing those people a bag of rocks.

Sadly, it is true that many pastors are poorly compensated by their congregations. There is an old saying about pastoral compensation that goes like this, "*Lord, you keep him humble, and we will keep him poor.* " This is a wicked, ungodly philosophy, and it is contrary to what the Bible teaches. Being poorly compensated, however, does not give a pastor a license to be a poor steward. He should exercise the care for and use of everything God has entrusted to his care, no matter how little or how much that is.

Congregations should be taught and encouraged to reward their spiritual overseer in a way that honors God. Failure to teach that truth cascades into the failure to care for the pastor. Paul told Timothy to teach them this truth: *"Let the elders who rule well be counted worthy of double honor, especially those who labor in the word and doctrine* (1 Timothy 5:17)." Do you think Timothy's blood pressure rose when he read this? Did the beads of sweat form on his brow? A faithful, Word-teaching pastor is of great value, and should be honored and compensated as such.

PERSONAL ACCOUNTABILITY

The most important reason for learning biblical stewardship is that he will one day give account to God for his own life, and for his ministry to others. It would be a wonderful thing for a pastor, near the end of his life and ministry, to be able to agree with the Apostle Paul, when he said, *"I have fought the good fight, I have finished the race, I have kept the faith. Finally, there is laid up for me the crown of righteousness, which the Lord, the righteous Judge, will give to me on that Day, and not to me only but also to all who have loved His appearing* (2 Timothy 4:7-8)."

I have learned in my personal study that if I am writing something that will be read by others, or if I am studying to preach a sermon that will be heard by others, my depth of study and desire for the truth is intensified. I want to be accurate about what God says. My conviction is strong after this kind of pursuit of truth, and so my faith is stronger, too.

So, we have seen that first of all there is much personal benefit for a pastor to learn and teach biblical stewardship. It is also of great benefit to others.

MINISTRY TO MEN

The pastor should learn and teach biblical stewardship for his personal ministry to men. The pastor's work in this area is about leadership. Consider the impact of the truth in this verse in today's world. Jesus had to exhort His disciples about the Pharisees who struggled to accept the teachings of Jesus. He told His disciples to *"let them alone. They are blind leaders of the blind. And if the blind leads the blind, both will fall into a ditch* (Matthew 15:14)." Do you see any of the men in your flock living in the proverbial ditch because of poor money management? Men who are blind to the biblical principles of financial stewardship? What does a pastor do when he sees men in a stewardship ditch? Does he let them stay there? Or does he speak the truth in love to deliver them?

The Pastor must know where (and to what) he is leading his men. His work as a pastor could be generally characterized as helping men become and remain qualified for positions of ministry (Titus 1). Whether or not God calls the men to vocational ministry is not the issue. Every man should desire and work toward being qualified as a servant leader. The man is going to lead his family, and so a pastor must help him do so by teaching principles and practices that are consistent with the ways of God. The man should also be able to teach stewardship to his own family. One day, his children will become leaders too. It becomes quite obvious that if a parent fails in this area, the failure becomes generational! Bad cycles of poverty and want are produced. I know what that is like; I grew up in one of those cycles! I did not like it!

Because the pastor is comfortable in the area of financial stewardship, he will understand and be able to communicate with businessmen in the congregation. Not only would this strengthen the men, but it would build his relationship with them. Business people seem to be in constant need of biblical counsel, as they experience the same temptations and are engaged on the same front lines of the culture that the unsaved face in this world. They are constantly both engaged in financial issues and influenced by ungodly thoughts and examples of worldly wealth management. Meeting with business people in their environment is much different than a discussion in the church lobby or the pastor's office.

Just because someone is a businessman does not mean they are a good manager of money. They are likely good at their business, but maybe not good at managing the revenues the business generates or the expenses it incurs. For example, maybe a man is a great chef or cook. That does not mean he knows how to run a restaurant efficiently and effectively. I have found in my ministry that many doctors generate a lot of revenue, but many have difficulty managing it. As a result, they are vulnerable to fraud and crippling debt.

A pastor's work is critical if the businessmen in the

congregation he shepherds are to "partner" with ministry by the exercising of their gifts. Remember, making disciples is relational, not programming.

Ministry to Couples

The pastor's knowledge and skill in the practice of biblical stewardship will also impact his ministry to couples. He can be considered as a vital link in God's "preventative maintenance program" for marriages. One of the leading factors that lead to divorce, and the number one reason pastors are counseling couples, is financial tension created by mismanaging God's money, causing marital problems. Oftentimes this mismanagement comes from ignorance, and other times from disobedience. In either scenario, the pastor has some responsibility, and it is a great opportunity to help the couple. If the pastor is not confident in this area, he will miss many of these opportunities. The preventative maintenance is regularly teaching the truth, even about finances!

Two key issues in a marriage when it comes to money are communication and unity. Biblical instruction and open discussion can set both parties on the same course of action with the same attitude, both of them pulling in the same direction. This certainly helps the couple grow.

Very few things cause one to question another's integrity in a greater way than unanswered questions about the family finances. Transparency and honesty are key communication issues. They help provide the unity that is so important to healthy marriages. It is quite common in today's culture that a couple ends up with a "my money, your money, and our money" philosophy. Perhaps each has their own bank accounts. Do you think the devil would plant the seeds of distrust in the couple's life because he would love to destroy the marriage? No doubt about it! It would serve a couple well to view their financial resources as "God's money under their care and management."

Ministry to Teenagers

A Pastor's good stewardship will also impact his ministry to teenagers. I want to mention just a couple of key points here. The teen needs to learn early the importance of good financial stewardship. They need to understand contentment, the pitfalls of debt, the positive influence of compounding, cash management, tithing, and a litany of other significant issues. It is certainly the parent's job to teach and train their children in this area. A pastor's sound teaching and preaching about financial issues will strengthen the parent's work with their children.

Another key is to provide instruction to teens as they begin to contemplate marriage. Many of them will come to the pastor for premarital counseling. I have heard many pastors tell young people to "seek the will of God about who your mate should be." Good advice for sure, but what does that mean to a teen? Should the teen pray, "Lord, is this one right for me?" and then wait for the "feeling?" I think not! Feelings often lead to foolishness. Where is a young person to get criteria to help them discern the will of God? How about the Bible! For example, 1 Timothy 5:8, although in context speaking about the care of widows, has some excellent principles that could be viewed as criteria to help in this process.

A young lady could ask, "Does the young man have a plan to provide for a wife and kids? Is he a man of the Word? Does he obey the Word of God now? Does he demonstrate this kind of responsibility now? Is he diligent or lazy when it concerns issues that will impact his future?"

These same thoughts could help a young man understand his responsibilities as he considers his own readiness to take a wife. Does he understand the relationship between work and provision? Is he open to hearing ideas or input from others, or is he too proud to listen to others' advice? How does he act toward his mother, or the mother of his future spouse? If he has little respect for them now, what will his care for them be later?

While the parents should be instructing their children about these issues, there is much in this area that a pastor can do to help the "flock of God" he is overseeing for the Great Shepherd. Not just teaching, preaching, and counseling, but also by setting a wonderful example.

Ministry to the Church

And finally, the pastor needs to learn biblical financial stewardship and teach it regularly for the sake of the churches in which he ministers. He should be able to understand the fiscal matters of the church as a corporate body. It will impact his leadership and vision and will impact the way folks follow his leadership. He would be able to understand and communicate better regarding the support of a mission's program. He could lead better as churches considered their ability to expand their outreach. It would also impact the Christian education aspect of the church's ministry. Financial resources can impact the quality and degree of this education in both positive and negative ways. For example, I learned as the director of a Bible camp that camping ministry is a wonderful context for promoting spiritual growth. That is a good thing. However, the camping ministry is labor intensive, but not revenue intensive. Camps just cannot generate the revenue they need to operate. They typically need financial partners to advance the ministry. Christian education is much the same—labor intensive but not revenue intensive. Because class sizes are limited, growing the student population is not the answer. Adding students means you have to add teachers. It can be a restrictive cycle of financial frustration.

I would offer this thought too: if I were a pastor, I would not want to be the person who managed all the financial transactions of the church. There is too much room for controversy, accusation, and temptation in doing so. It can destroy a pastor's ministry. The church should be totally transparent about financial affairs as they have a testimony to protect, and that testimony is the great name of God.

If it seems like the influence and impact of money has great significance on a pastor, then the pastor should better understand why he needs to invest the time to learn biblical financial stewardship. He should plan regular time to "keep fresh" in this area. Although he need not be a financial expert or guru, he should have some basic understanding of the tools and resources available to help people practice good stewardship. I suspect that one of the best ways to do that would be to begin to minister to others about their personal financial stewardship. Whenever we are in a "real-life" disciple-making context and questions arise, our learning fervor is elevated significantly, and our ability to teach is strengthened. Consider the tragic condition of those to whom the writer of Hebrews pens these words,

> For though by this time you ought to be teachers, you need someone to teach you again the first principles of the oracles of God; and you have come to need milk and not solid food. For everyone who partakes only of milk is unskilled in the word of righteousness, for he is a babe. But solid food belongs to those who are of full age, that is, those who by reason of use have their senses exercised to discern both good and evil.
> (Hebrews 5:12-14)

The writer is exhorting an audience of people who had been saved long enough, and taught well enough, that they should have been teaching the basic, principled truth of the Christian life to other people. However, before they would be able to do this, someone would have to come in and "re-teach" them the basics before they could ever teach them to another. Their capacity to learn and communicate was likened to the digestion capacity of a baby in need of milk rather than that of someone who was fully mature and able to digest meat. There is an important lesson to learn here: *"If you don't use it, you lose it!"* Continual use and engagement keep one fresh in their understanding of truth and their ability to teach or counsel others.

As you can see, it is very important for a pastor to have a good understanding of the Biblical teaching of financial stewardship. It is especially important for a pastor since he is to minister to those who possess wealth. Without having a critical spirit about this issue, I will tell you that I have ministered in many small churches across the country where there were few, if any, wealthy people. I often wonder if that is not the result of a pastor's reluctance or sense of inadequacy to address financial matters, and so those in need of the teaching and counsel seek another ministry or minister to help them with this significant responsibility.

CHAPTER 4

THE STEWARD'S PRIMARY RESPONSIBILITY

THE GLORY OF GOD

THE STEWARD'S PRIMARY RESPONSIBILITY IS TO GLORIFY GOD with his life by doing God's will on earth, not his own will. Early in his instruction to his disciples, Jesus taught this important lesson:

> *You are the light of the world. A city that is set on a hill cannot be hidden. Nor do they light a lamp and put it under a basket, but on a lampstand, and it gives light to all who are in the house. Let your light so shine before men, that they may see your good works and glorify your Father in heaven.* (Matthew 5:14-16)

My wife and I were having dinner with a Christian couple after I preached one Sunday morning in the church they attended. Both the husband and wife were from Lebanon and were now medical doctors practicing in the city where they were currently living. They had a wonderful family. As we were finishing up, the conversation having turned to the things of God, the lady asked an interesting question: "Why didn't God take us immediately to be with Him in heaven when He saved us?" Jesus' teaching here gives us great insight into the mind of God regarding that question. As believers, we are placed in this world by Christ to be a light that shines in the darkness. As people observe our lives (that is, our light), what they see should cause them to form an opinion of the God we serve. A primary responsibility of every believer is to live their life in such a way that, as others observe them, it projects into the minds of the observers an accurate opinion of God, both of His person and His character. This is what it means to glorify God. Paul expanded on this when he wrote to the church at Corinth.

> *Therefore, whether you eat or drink, or whatever you do, do all to the glory of God. Give no offense, either to the Jews or to the Greeks or to the church of God, just as I also please all men in all things, not seeking my own profit, but the profit of many, that they may be saved.* (1 Corinthians 10:31-33)

As people observed the children of God and began to form an opinion based on their behavior, the character of God being lived out through these followers of Jesus would help people see their own sinfulness and need for a Savior. Paul clearly stated the desired outcome, *"that they may be saved."*

In the following excerpt from the Apostle Paul's letter to Pastor Timothy, Paul exhorts the pastor to address four key areas regarding the Christian's management of the resources of wealth and riches God would entrust to any person. First, their ATTITUDE about wealth, then their ACTIVITY with their wealth, followed by the ACCOMPLISHMENT of proper stewardship of the wealth God gave them to manage, and finally, the AVOIDANCE of faith-destroying opposition. The following is the text of Paul's letter to Timothy exhorting him to this end:

> *Command those who are rich in this present age not to be haughty, nor to trust in uncertain riches but in the living God, who gives us richly all things to enjoy. Let them do good, that they be rich in good works, ready to give, willing to share, storing up for themselves a good foundation for the time to come, that they may lay hold on eternal life.*
>
> *O Timothy! Guard what was committed to your trust, avoiding the profane and idle babblings and contradictions of what is falsely called knowledge—by professing it some have strayed concerning the faith. Grace be with you. Amen.*
> (I Timothy 6:17-21)

From this passage, one can understand the ways of God regarding the management of wealth, and, through obedience to God's will and practicing God's way, one can be an example and project an accurate opinion of both the person and character of God. That is what "glorifying God" would look like in the daily living of a biblical steward as they managed the master's stuff, including the wealth beyond their personal need they have been entrusted to steward.

Let us take a deeper look into each of these exhortations in the next chapters.

CHAPTER 5

THE ATTITUDE
OF THE STEWARD

ATTITUDE IS IMPORTANT. A POSITIVE ATTITUDE CAN BE the strength one needs to get through a challenging time. A negative attitude can snatch defeat from the jaws of victory. An attitude not only influences what we do, but it also makes a difference in how we do it. Solomon said, "*For as he thinks in his heart, so is he* (Proverbs 23:7a)." In other words, attitude determines action.

It will be especially important for the biblical steward to maintain the right attitude about their stewardship. The world, the flesh, and the devil will do all they can to distort or undermine the godly attitude of the servant of God. One way this happens is by applying constant pressure to assume the role of an owner instead of being a steward. This pressure can be subtle, but it is still pressure.

The reward a steward receives in heaven is determined not

only by what he does, but also by why he did it the way he did. In other words, "Did he have the right attitude?" Motives matter to God. Attitudes are important. So, consider each phrase in verse seventeen to get a greater understanding of the right attitude of a steward.

"Charge Them That Are Rich in This World!"

The apostle's exhortation to Pastor Timothy was absolutely necessary. Approaching wealthy people is difficult enough, but talking about their wealth can take a pastor's anxiety to a higher level. Timothy would need and appreciate the apostle's encouragement. Remember, pastors like Timothy are under-shepherds of the Great Shepherd Jesus Christ. They have a responsibility to speak the truth to the flock which God has commanded them to oversee. "*Therefore take heed to yourselves and to all the flock, among which the Holy Spirit has made you overseers, to shepherd the church of God which He purchased with His own blood* (Acts 20:28)." As we have already stated, sometimes this task becomes uncomfortable for a pastor.

All of God's sheep should remain open to biblical instruction and exhortation because the Bible tells us we need God's leadership in our lives. As we previously mentioned, Jeremiah the Prophet of God, speaking to the House of Israel, once declared, "*O LORD, I know the way of man is not in himself; It is not in man who walks to direct his own steps. O LORD, correct me, but with justice; Not in Your anger, lest You bring me to nothing* (Jeremiah 10:23-24)." Jeremiah was acknowledging that the capacity for man to both successfully direct his own way through life and accomplish

God's will for his life just is not there! How humbling is that? Especially for someone who has accomplished much in life. We need the leading and guiding of God. Let this truth sink in for a minute. It is so important and yet so antithetical to the mindset of most people, which is evidenced by man's unwillingness to ask for help or to receive instruction. "I'll do it my way!" is a common mindset.

The Psalmist wrote, "*The steps of a good man are ordered by the LORD: and He delights in his way* (Psalm 37:23)." God's Word guiding man's heart by the Holy Spirit will direct the steps a man should take. And the grace of God is what empowers a man to obediently take those steps, fulfilling God's will.

It was Timothy's responsibility to minister the truth of God's Word to those who held riches and wealth. They must use their riches responsibly if they were to be rich in the age to come. It is the steward's responsibility to be open to the instruction and admonition from the spiritual leaders God has placed in their lives. It's how we grow spiritually.

In his testimony of his own transformational experience about his opinion of the rich, Pastor Steve Perry shares the following:

> "I actually rather liked it when I heard James thunder, *"Now listen, you rich people, weep and wail because of the misery that is coming upon you. Your wealth has rotted, and moths have eaten your clothes. Your gold and silver are corroded. Their corrosion will testify against you and eat your flesh like fire"* (James 5:1–3). But I never bothered to notice that James directed his scathing

rebukes not to "rich people" in general, but to those who had "hoarded wealth," to those who had "failed to pay the workmen who mowed your fields," to those who had "lived on earth in luxury and self-indulgence" and who "condemned and murdered innocent men, who were not opposing you." Such men had "fattened" themselves for "the day of slaughter," James predicted (verses 3–6). Hooray! But what was I to do with a God who would say to a band of ancient Christians, *"You will be made rich in every way so that you can be generous on every occasion, and through us your generosity will result in thanksgiving to God"* (2 Corinthians 9:11- NIV)? I really didn't know. But unknown to me, I would soon find out."[5]

Consider this statement from the *Homiletic Commentary on 1 Timothy, chapter VI*:

> *"To lavish wealth on personal luxuries is to abuse it and ourselves. On the statue of Joseph Brotherton is the inscription, "A man's riches consist not in the amount of his wealth, but in the fewness of his wants."*

I do not think the commentator was condemning riches, rather that he was pointing out the danger of misuse and/or misunderstanding them. Rich people can have a level of contentment that is not the effect of, or affected by, the wealth they possess. Their contentment is in the person of Christ and their position in Him.

"THAT THEY BE NOT HIGH MINDED."

In this second phrase, we learn that riches have the power to deceive man into thinking more highly of himself than he should. Paul wrote to the believers in Rome, "*For I say, through the grace given to me, to everyone who is among you, not to think of himself more highly than he ought to think, but to think soberly, as God has dealt to each one a measure of faith* (Romans 12:3)." Our egos can lead us astray very quickly. We have a natural inclination to compete and establish prominence or dominance over others by lifting ourselves up. This is one of the effects of pride. We must guard against developing this attitude because the potential is inherent in the possession of wealth.

Pride is an ever-present danger to those with riches. One can believe they "are" more because they "have" more than another man has. In a sense, it is their identity. The Apostle Paul writing to the churches of Galatia reminded them about humility when he wrote, "*For if anyone thinks himself to be something, when he is nothing, he deceives himself* (Galatians 6:3)."

Practically speaking, we see wealth and riches have the power to convince one to divide people into classes, or levels of significance or importance. It is common to hear someone speak of the "lower class,' or the "middle class,' or the "ruling elite class.' God is no respecter of persons (see Acts 10:34). God does not put us into these classes. They are man-made divisions, and this issue is a real battle for many. It is the battle of self-exaltation. Money is often the fuel behind such thinking.

And consider also how quick we are to take credit for the

successes we have experienced in life. We think it was our great skill, or our extraordinary effort that accomplished something great. We take credit because we worked hard, or took the risk, or assembled the right team. We view ourselves as "experienced,' or "experts!' But God's Word has something to say about this that brings one "back to earth,' so to speak! Moses, exhorting God's people who would experience great blessing, wrote:

> *Beware that you do not forget the LORD your God by not keeping His commandments, His judgments, and His statutes which I command you today, lest—when you have eaten and are full, and have built beautiful houses and dwell in them; and when your herds and your flocks multiply, and your silver and your gold are multiplied, and all that you have is multiplied; when your heart is lifted up, and you forget the LORD your God who brought you out of the land of Egypt, from the house of bondage; who led you through that great and terrible wilderness, in which were fiery serpents and scorpions and thirsty land where there was no water; who brought water for you out of the flinty rock; who fed you in the wilderness with manna, which your fathers did not know, that He might humble you and that He might test you, to do you good in the end—then you say in your heart, 'My power and the might of my hand have gained me this wealth.'*

> *And you shall remember the LORD your God, for it is He who gives you power to get wealth, that He may establish His covenant which He swore to your fathers, as it is this day. Then it shall be, if you by any means forget the LORD your*

*God, and follow other gods, and serve them and worship them,
I testify against you this day that you shall surely perish. As
the nations which the LORD destroys before you, so you shall
perish, because you would not be obedient to the voice of the
LORD your God.* (Deuteronomy 8:11-20)

God's plan for his people went way beyond the personal success of an individual. He had a master plan for the ages and these people had the privilege of being part of it. It is so easy for us to get so wrapped up in our own little world that we, too, forget the bigger picture, and the bigger person.

God is the one that gives man the ability to work and make money. He provides us with the opportunities, the strength, the time, and the talents or abilities to accomplish this process. He does so to advance his plan, fulfilling the covenants He made. It is especially important for those with riches to stay humble and maintain a proper perspective on their wealth. And we should not miss the priority God places on this issue by mentioning it first.

"Nor Trust in Uncertain Riches, but in the Living God."

In this next phrase there is an interesting adjective that Paul uses to describe riches. They are "uncertain." The value of, or the possession of, riches is certainly uncertain! History tells us that the stock market goes up and down like a roller coaster. Inflation can begin suddenly and accelerate very quickly. What is worth something today can be worthless tomorrow!

I had a personal experience with this devaluation issue. When my father passed away in the mid-1990s I was the recipient of his Norman Rockwell collection of limited-edition figurines. The appraiser of dad's estate valued them at $25,000. Today that collection is worth very little. The markets changed, the demand diminished, and the value declined!

Wealth can disappear quickly. A company or a bank can collapse overnight and leave the investors or depositors holding an empty bag. The thief or the swindler can strip one of their wealth in a heartbeat. Scam artists are constantly preying on the elderly, who they presume have accumulated wealth, and can empty a bank account with the click of a mouse. Realities like this are why Paul exhorts Pastor Timothy to remind those with wealth of its uncertainty.

While we must value riches, we must understand they are not worthy of putting one's trust or confidence into them. Paul exhorts Timothy to remind the believers to keep their faith and trust in the living God. Think of the contrast here! Money and riches are quite temporary, both in their existence and endurance. On the other hand, the living God is eternal and all powerful. His resources are unlimited and forever. He is worthy of our trust and confidence! And here is a great blessing: He is the one with the capacity and desire to meet our needs.

King David, as the Psalmist, warned us, *"Do not trust in oppression, nor vainly hope in robbery; if riches increase, do not set your heart on them (Psalm 62:10)."*

While wealth can be a great tool, it can also become a

great enemy in our walk of faith if we allow it to undermine our reliance on God. Depend on God! He loves you. He saved you. He adopted you into His family. And He wants to, and has promised, to meet your needs. Our difficulty comes when our desires and/or understanding is in conflict with God's plan.

Trusting God is not a journey of foolish irresponsibility! We all admire the stories of George Müller and his orphanage, and the miraculous provision God made for this man. It is certainly God's prerogative to do the miraculous. That's His job. Faith is taking God at His word and acting upon it. That is our job. We need to learn the principles of stewardship well and faithfully put them to practice in our lives, trusting God for a right outcome—His blessing. And if He chooses the miraculous for us, then praise the Lord!

It should not escape us that many of God's choice servants were stewards of great wealth—Joseph, David, Solomon, and others. Consider the following from the *Homiletic Commentary: I Timothy, chapter VI*:

> *Riches are given for use, not for storage. The moment we begin to selfishly store them, we begin to trust in them. Money is a circulating medium, and its true value is in its wise and judicious circulation. Our use of money is part of our education in life and needs as much care and thought as the business that produces it. God only, and not wealth, maintains the world: riches not properly used only make people proud and lazy. To trust in riches is committing ourselves to a great uncertainty.*

"Who Giveth Us Richly All Things to Enjoy."

Not only does God want to advance His plan for mankind by having stewards effectively manage His stuff, but God wants the steward to enjoy the process too. It is so easy to lose sight of the desire of Jesus for us when He said, "*These things I have spoken to you, that My joy may remain in you, and that your joy may be full* (John 15:11)." As we abide in Him, and He accomplishes His work through us, we experience that joy! What a deal! God feels strongly about our participation, as is evidenced by His giving "richly' all things. We serve a generous Master! He cares about us!

Whenever I read this phrase, my mind goes immediately to the words of the Apostle Paul as he speaks to the elders of Ephesus. He quotes the Lord Jesus when he says, "*I have shown you in every way, by laboring like this, that you must support the weak. And remember the words of the Lord Jesus, that He said, 'It is more blessed to give than to receive'* (Acts 20:35)." Mankind, in his selfish nature, loves receiving things. But learning to give, and being active in doing so, brings joy and happiness that far exceeds "getting" something. It also guards us from materialism and putting our trust in uncertain riches.

Being a husband, father, grandfather, and now a great-grandfather, I can really relate to this truth. I would much rather give gifts to my wife, children, or grandchildren than have them give gifts to me. And this is not unlike our Heavenly Father and His desire toward us as His children. He loves us for who we are, not what we do! And so, He gives us richly so we can enjoy all that He has for us.

This truth is so misunderstood, and seldom taught, that it can lead to a wrong perception of who God is. God is not a stingy old ogre who is seeking to inflict as much difficulty and pain on mankind as He can. He is a tender, loving Father who wants to bless His children. He knows our happiness will come from knowing who He really is, and from learning and doing His will, not by accumulating temporal treasures that may distract us from having a loving relationship with Him. His attention and approval surpass all that is earthly.

So, verse seventeen is directed toward the believer's attitude about the wealth and riches God entrusts to their care as a steward. Having the right thinking and the right attitude will help us to do the right thing! And understanding God's desire to be rich toward His children is so encouraging. This is such a positive thought, and it provides the power that motivates us as we journey through life. This encourages me as a possessor of wealth.

CHAPTER 6

THE ACTIVITY
OF THE STEWARD

ONCE WE HAVE THE PROPER ATTITUDE ABOUT WEALTH and riches, then we can focus on our activity with it. This is the next portion of Paul's exhortation to Timothy. Verse eighteen gives us four phrases that go a long way toward providing understanding for what the direction of our activity with wealth should be: *"Let them do good, that they be rich in good works, ready to give, willing to share."* Let us look at each of these phrases individually.

"LET THEM DO GOOD."

The idea here is engaging in virtuous (or good) work. This is a characterization of the activity itself. As one learns the will of God, they will discover that doing the will of God will involve engaging in virtuous activities. It is work that is both beneficial to mankind and praiseworthy to God. Anything other than that should raise a red flag for the steward. But be careful here. It characterizes the work, not necessarily the context, in which the work is being done. Remember, Jesus was criticized for meeting and eating with sinners.

This requires one to exercise discretion when opportunities come their way. Not every opportunity would be good, and God may not have you involved in some of those good opportunities, either. For example, I served as the director of a Christian Bible camp ministry for twelve years and had responsibility for the operations and development of the ministry. This included sharing needs and opportunities so we could have the funds needed to advance the work.

One of the great lessons I learned in this role was that different people are interested in supporting or funding different things. Some wanted to build buildings. Some wanted to support our staff. Others wanted to provide scholarships for campers to experience a week of Bible camp. And there was a good explanation for this diversity. God would lay burdens for these unique needs on the heart of the people, and the people, recognizing this work of God in their hearts, exercised good stewardship and gave specifically to the needs they believed God would have them meet. Although this does not sound so difficult to understand, we do see the importance of our faith walk in the process. The possession of wealth is meant for good because its owner is good! The owner has an agenda for how it is to be used, and the work is virtuous.

Allow me to share one example of my own growth in understanding a little more of how God works in this manner.

One Saturday morning, as a grueling week of teen camp was ending (the campers were gone, the staff was finishing up their responsibilities, and all of us were tired and looking forward to a few hours of rest), a middle-aged couple came into the camp office. Our receptionist came to me and said there was a couple who wanted to talk to me about helping in the camp. For illustration's sake, and to honor their desire, I will use an alias and call them Bob and Betty. As they were ushered into my office, at first glance, and in my cynicism, I thought to myself, "Oh, I'll bet she wants to help cook and he wants to mow the grass."

After the introductions, the couple sat down and we began our discussion. They were quite interested in how the recent week had gone and commented on how they loved the camp and the work that was done there. Their grown children had attended the camp as young people.

I asked, "How can we help you?"

Then Bob said, "We would like to help out here."

To which I responded, "Wonderful, we welcome volunteers!" That response really exposed my dismissive mindset. Looking back on the incident now, I was probably tired and a bit impatient. I thought the people were looking for something to do.

Then Bob began to ask some more probing questions about our plans, our purpose, and how the work was going overall. He asked me about my vision for the coming years. Before long, and after assessing my answers, Bob said, "We would like to begin our help by providing for the development of a master plan for the property." After some discussion, I would understand that that would include an aerial survey of all 180 acres to understand the topography, the placing structures,

75

and so on. Bob's thinking was way beyond what mine was at the moment.

What I came to find out is that this is what God had laid on Bob and Betty's hearts. They were successful business people who were generating capital and they wanted to help advance the kingdom of God. They saw this as their role, their part in God's plan. They ended up investing tens of thousands of dollars in this project, and it was of great value to the camp. It was a great lesson for me.

I also served as the Director of Development at a Bible college for several years. The financial needs at institutions like these are great, and so we developed initiatives to appeal to major donors and asked them to give prayerful consideration about participating in the funding of these initiatives. I learned from a wise man who God brought into my path that there are three key issues that major donors consider when determining philanthropic gifting.

First, they want to give to a cause in which they believe. In a sense, this is a "values proposition." They ask themselves, "Is this a cause in which God would have me participate?" Typically, God has placed a burden on the heart of the steward that resulted in them having interest in particular types of projects or opportunities, and thus the cause presented had "donor appeal." The institution was not responsible for creating the "donor appeal," it was responsible for communicating accurately the need they recognized. It would be God who would make it appealing to His steward.

And then one might ask, "Do I sense God's leading in this opportunity?" This is where prayer plays a key role. What is the

Holy Spirit's rule in their heart impressing on them to do? We want them to determine their participation by the will of God, not from the appeal of a man or the emotions stimulated by a perceived need. The steward must beware, because the clever marketers of the world are highly skilled at making emotional appeals or developing emergency crises. This really is a gold, silver, and precious stones issue. Wood, hay, and stubble have no eternal benefit. Why the donor gave to the cause is the key issue here. Remember, motive matters.

Second, the biblical steward of significant wealth wants to see leadership they can trust. What has this leader accomplished in the past? What are they trying to accomplish now and why? Getting answers to these questions usually necessitates a face-to-face relationship between the leadership and the donors. The philanthropists can get information "straight from the horse's mouth," which is important for their understanding the vision for the future and developing confidence that the leadership needs to fulfill the vision. As a friend once said, "I want to look them in the eye. It seems to be the window to their soul." This statement illustrates the importance of the personal relationship in philanthropy.

One thing this taught me is that the donor is not simply making a gift to an organization or person; they, at His direction, are investing in the plan of God.

Third and finally, they want to see organizational stewardship that is practiced with excellence and transparency. Since the steward is both practicing stewardship and wants their stewardship to be approved by God, exercising due diligence regarding the stewardship of the recipient organization will be important. How someone uses and cares for what they already have will play a major role in this process of discernment. Excellence is a characteristic of God, and the donor wants to see it in the cause they are supporting. It projects the right opinion!

Transparency will be a critical issue too. If a ministry or organization is hiding some aspect of their operation or financial activity, it will provide a red flag to the prospective donor. One must understand that wealth certainly holds the capacity to enable its possessor to do terrible things with it too. Perhaps you have heard scenarios like the following: a person is caught doing something wrong or inappropriate and they are asked, "Why did you do this?" Their response is "Because I could." Wealth became an enabler to do something they should not do.

When considering stewardship opportunities, one should use the Bible to help determine whether this was a good or bad opportunity. Is the work something God would bless? Or is the work something that would bring shame or criticism to the cause of Christ? The use of riches certainly requires discernment. Every cause and every need are not necessarily virtuous! Praying for God's leading and listening to the Holy Spirit while searching the Scriptures will be a profitable exercise for the believer as a steward of God's stuff.

"That They Be Rich in Good Works."

I find this second phrase in verse eighteen to be fascinating. The idea here is that one "becomes" rich in good works. In other words, this is a learned behavior. It must be learned because it is contrary to the selfish nature of man.

To help us understand this truth, let us consider the example of what Solomon taught to his son in Proverbs 19:17. His statement provides an amazing picture. He said, "*He who has pity on the poor lends to the LORD, and He will pay back what he has given.*" The picture Solomon paints with words is this: as one who has resources (for illustration's sake, let us call him John) comes upon another who is poor, meaning they have a need they cannot currently meet themselves (we will call him Joe), the one with riches, John, reaches out with his stuff, and gives it to meet the need Joe has. By John being ready, willing, and able to give, and then doing it, Joe's needs are met.

This act is described by Solomon as "lending to the Lord." How interesting! The Lord is the one who provided the resources to John, who is now giving them away to meet the needs of Joe. In doing so, Solomon says John is "lending to the Lord," meaning "to join in or twine."[6] We might ask ourselves, "Is John really lending the stuff, or is he lending himself by being usable and giving God's stuff to Joe?" I am not sure I can adequately answer that question, but it certainly makes one consider the process of meeting needs.

In the illustration, John is the conduit God chose to use. Could God have met Joe's needs directly, without involving John? Certainly! But He allowed John to be part of the process and experience the blessing. And so, we see that by engaging us in the process of meeting needs, God is allowing us to experience some of the same joy He feels when meeting someone's needs.

Now, think about this. Pretend you are John in the illustration. As you reach out, and empty your hands of your stuff to meet Joe's needs, how do you feel inside? Feels good, right? And then, as you draw your empty hands back to yourself, the Lord fills them again. How amazing is that? Now being given more resources, you get to experience this same process again with someone else in need. And just like before, it feels great to meet one's needs. And so, you engage in the next opportunity, and then the next, and then the next.

Before long, you find yourself saying, "I want to do this again! I want to do this more often! I want to do this in a bigger way!" What is happening? You are learning a new behavior. This is the point Paul is making to Timothy. People need to learn this behavior because it is antithetical to their selfish nature. Instead of being stingy, or simply indifferent, we should become a distributor of God's stuff. It is a wonderful thing to be used by God to meet the needs of others! So join in!

"READY TO GIVE"

This third phrase carries the idea of being a "ready distributor" of their riches. One has an easier time doing this when they have the right thinking regarding their responsibility. As a steward of God's stuff and ordering their life in submission to the will of God, one can easily "let go" of the riches, knowing it is the Master Who is fulfilling His agenda through them (Who, by the way, has an unlimited supply of resources). And, as we learned earlier, there is a great blessing for the one who gives.

The steward's generous participation in the process of God meeting the needs of others brings great happiness and joy. And because of our learned experience, we expect God to continue using us. This makes it much easier to maintain a light grip on what we possess. This is what the trendy phrase "Let go, and let God" would really look like. Implied here though, is letting go of stuff, not just dismissing a circumstance. There is a huge difference!

"WILLING TO SHARE"

I must admit that this fourth little phrase is where the plot thickens. Being willing to share in this context has the idea of becoming a liberal distributor who is looking to "partner up." This moves the concept of generous giving from passive behavior to proactive behavior. In *Strong's Concordance of the Bible*, the language used to describe this behavior is this: "inclined to make others to be sharers in one's possessions, inclined to impart, free in giving, liberal."[7]

This means the possessor of riches should be partnering intentionally to advance the master's agenda. They have sought God's leadership and are now seeking to execute the direction they have received from the Lord. To me, this is an amazing concept, and highly motivating. It completely answers the question with which many struggle: "Why do I have all this wealth when others do not?" Some people actually feel guilty for possessing wealth or riches. They need not feel this way! It is God who has entrusted the care for, and use of, some of His stuff to them as a faithful manager. So, the exhortation should be this: "Be one!"

It seems to me that the lack of understanding in the activity often results in those with riches getting caught up in the hamster wheel of selfishness by pursuing "bigger and better." We spend all our riches on advancing our own standard of living and fulfilling the ever-growing "bucket list." And having counseled many people in this area, I have learned that enough never seems to be enough. This is such a temporal view of riches, and quite commonly found in the life of a Christian. This is what becomes "wood, hay, and stubble."

So often in the world of fundraising or institutional advancement the wealthy are bombarded with requests for funding. These requests are often poorly planned and poorly presented. The possessor of the wealth must spend much time researching and discerning the requests, seeking to determine which ones would be the will of God for their stewardship. They narrow their choices and select some to fund and reject the other requests. They reject funding far more than they fund. What a negative and discouraging experience that can be for the philanthropist! Their exercise of stewardship seems to be more reactive than proactive and becomes discouraging instead of encouraging. In fact, it becomes a great burden.

There is danger here for which we must provide a word of caution. If this pattern of being reactive becomes their exclusive experience for the possessor of riches, then the steward could begin to view the requesters as "beggars coming to the king" to have their needs met. Giving in to the temptation here would be a form of self-exaltation. It is the first thing about which Paul told Timothy to warn the wealthy.

A proactive approach to partnering would involve seeking and discerning God's will regarding the use and distribution of resources that had been entrusted to them. This might result in the formulation of a purpose or vision statement and then pursuing opportunities that fit that cause. The steward would not only engage in managing and distributing money, but they would also be diligently pursuing the advancement of organizations or causes that fit their vision.

I would not discount the possibility that a combination of proactive and reactive stewardship would be the will of God and could result in a proper balance.

CHAPTER 7

THE ACCOMPLISHMENT OF THE STEWARD

TIMOTHY IS TO CHARGE THOSE WHO POSSESS RICHES in this life to have the right attitude about this responsibility and opportunity. He is to exhort them as to their activity with their riches and wealth. And now, in verse nineteen, he addresses the accomplishment of practicing good stewardship. Paul writes, "*storing up for themselves a good foundation for the time to come, that they may lay hold on eternal life.*" It seems to me that there are two major themes in this verse.

"LAYING UP TREASURE IN HEAVEN"

The first accomplishment is "investing in eternity," or laying up treasure in Heaven. By having the right attitude and activity, the possessor of riches is laying a good foundation against the time to come. The question is, "Of what time is he speaking?" It could be the latter time that Paul wrote of in chapter four, where some would depart from the faith, having been seduced by spirits and doctrines of devils. Some have suggested it is the "perilous time" that Paul would write about in his second letter. The author believes the time Paul speaks of is the "appearing of our Lord Jesus Christ" he writes of in this same chapter, saying: *"I urge you in the sight of God who gives life to all things, and before Christ Jesus who witnessed the good confession before Pontius Pilate, that you keep this commandment without spot, blameless until our Lord Jesus Christ's appearing* (1 Timothy 6:13-14)."

God's Word teaches us that good stewardship will be rewarded at the Judgment Seat of Christ. *"For we must all appear before the judgment seat of Christ, that each one may receive the things done in the body, according to what he has done, whether good or bad* (2 Corinthians 5:10)." As one understands the will of God regarding their stewardship, and exercises it with the right attitude, understanding, and motivation, it builds toward the reward.

Remember, Paul told the Corinthian believers in 1 Corinthians 3 that, as co-laborers with God, they needed to be careful how they built upon the foundation that was previously laid in the work they were furthering, because every man's work would be made manifest. Would it stand the judgment by fire and come forth as gold, silver, and precious stones, or would it be burned up and to no avail, like wood, hay, and stubble?

It will be an amazing thing to see our earthly investments stand the fiery tests of this judgment. Can you imagine the joy one will experience when they realize they have pleased their Lord by practicing good stewardship? What greater compliment could one expect to hear than *"Well done, good and faithful steward."*

And allow me to plant a seed of thought that may drive you to do some additional study. I find it interesting how God uses incentives in our lives. From the Garden of Eden to the Judgment Seat of Christ, you see this. God does not force us to violate the free will He has given us, rather He provides incentives for us to do the right thing. He wants us to choose to love Him, and He wants us to choose to serve Him. Consider the last two verses in the Bible and notice the incentive: *"He who testifies to these things says, 'Surely I am coming quickly.' Amen. Even so, come, Lord Jesus! The grace of our Lord Jesus Christ be with you all. Amen* (Revelation 22:20-21)." He is coming! And He is coming soon!

"LAYING HOLD ON ETERNAL LIFE"

The second theme is "laying hold on eternal life." Do not miss the importance of this phrase. When some think of eternal life, the only thing they think about is: "I am going to Heaven when I die." While that is surely important, it is not the definition of eternal life. Jesus defines eternal life when He says: *"And this is eternal life, that they may know You, the only true God, and Jesus Christ whom You have sent* (John 17:3)."

Eternal life is having a living, knowledgeable relationship with God—NOW! The moment we are saved we have eternal life, and we have everlasting life. We have been born again! We have passed from death unto life! We are alive in Christ with access to the Father, Who wants to hear from us regularly and engage us continually.

Laying hold on this truth has the idea of "seizing it." Embracing with all our heart and our very being is what is being said. It is embracing your role as a steward instead of being the owner—making it a reality in your mind and a practice in your life. There is a very real sense that this is shifting one's focus from the temporal things of this world to the eternal things of God. It includes making sure you are in constant communication with God, the Creator and Sustainer of everything we possess. Through this kind of engagement, we will have the right perspective on the wealth and riches we have. This is the point Paul is making!

We will also understand that we possess these riches by God's grace. The power to care for them properly and use them for God's glory is found in God's grace. The word "grace" (verse twenty-one) speaks of God's "enablement." We are governed by God's controlling influence on our heart. He makes us able managers of His stuff! To me, this is some of what Jesus meant when He said we must lose our life to save it (see Luke 9:23-27 Christ's call to discipleship).

So, we understand our right thinking and right action will result in a wonderful reward. What an incentive! How motivating is that? What an incredible opportunity for the steward. What purpose it brings to one's life. Once again, consider an admonishment from the *Homiletic Commentary: I Timothy, chapter VI.*

> *To spend life in getting and keeping money is to be poor indeed; to spend it in a liberal use of our means in the cause of God is to be enriched with eternal life—which is life indeed.*

There is truth and instruction in the inscription on an Italian tombstone, "What I gave away I saved; what I spent I used; what I kept I lost."

The inscription made me think of missionary Jim Elliott's famous quote. He wrote in his journal on October 28, 1949, "*He is no fool who gives what he cannot keep to gain that which he cannot lose.*"[8] Elliott certainly understood he was a conduit, a tool in the hand of almighty God. He saw himself as a manager of God's stuff, and he was using it to advance the eternal kingdom of God.

CHAPTER 8

THE AVOIDANCES
OF THE STEWARD

AND FINALLY, PAUL WARNS TIMOTHY TO AVOID SOME things that would distract from or destroy one's good stewardship. "*O Timothy! Guard what was committed to your trust, avoiding the profane and idle babblings and contradictions of what is falsely called knowledge—by professing it some have strayed concerning the faith. Grace be with you. Amen* (1 Timothy 6:20-21)."

"PROFANE AND IDLE BABBLINGS"

Timothy was to avoid "profane and idle babblings," that is, ungodly or heathen discussion of fruitless and useless matters. Everyone has opinions and ideas. And when it comes to riches and wealth, the selfish nature of man can be highly creative and adamant. The steward must have the mind of Christ in the matters of managing the Master's resources.

Here is an example of one of these profane and vain babblings that I would be familiar with, "*God helps those who help themselves.*" This statement is often used to undermine the work of God in favor of the effort of man. Jesus, speaking as the Vine to the branches, reminds us of a humbling reality when He said, "*for without Me ye can do nothing* (John 15:5b)."

The Bible has much instruction on financial stewardship, both from a positive and negative perspective. Consider some of these instructive warnings:

"*He who has a slack hand becomes poor, but the hand of the diligent makes rich* (Proverbs 10:4)." Laziness instead of diligence is poor stewardship.

"*There is one who scatters, yet increases more; and there is one who withholds more than is right, but it leads to poverty* (Proverbs 11:24)." Stinginess instead of generosity is poor stewardship.

"*He who tills his land will be satisfied with bread, but he who follows frivolity is devoid of understanding* (Proverbs 12:11)." Chasing fantasies over virtuous work is poor stewardship.

"*Getting treasures by a lying tongue is the fleeting fantasy of those who seek death* (Proverbs 21:6)." Dishonesty is poor stewardship, fruitless, and destructive.

"*He who oppresses the poor to increase his riches, and he who gives to the rich, will surely come to poverty* (Proverbs 22:16)." Oppressing, or using the poor for personal gain, is poor stewardship.

"*A man with an evil eye hastens after riches, and does not consider that poverty will come upon him* (Proverbs 28:22)." Does "look before you leap" come to mind?

Remember, it is God's opinion and direction that is important to the steward, and there is wisdom in a multitude of counsel. If you are stuck or struggling, seek some godly counsel.

"Contradictions of What is Falsely Called Knowledge"

These oppositions of man's knowledge are conflicts or theories based on one's expressed knowledge that bear a false title or name. They are human learnings that get labeled as science in order to provide credibility to their claim. We are not "anti-science." Paul is simply warning of the misuse of science, or the scientific outcomes, that conflict with God's truth and are used to contend with God and His Word. They may be sincere in their presentation, but they are sincerely wrong in their conclusions. We understand that false prophets and false teachers may intentionally twist words or create new meanings for old words to create doubt and destroy confidence. That is how Satan deceived Adam and Eve in the Garden of Eden.

As previously mentioned, there are many so-called scientific ideas and theories that are in opposition to God's Word. Theories such as the big bang theory, the theory of evolution, and the ideas of spontaneous generation, cosmogenesis, and others are contrary to the teachings of the Bible. Embracing an idea or thing that is in contradiction to God's Word is akin to giving the enemy a beachfront from which he can launch other attacks on one's faith.

The point that Paul makes to Timothy in these warnings is this; these things, if not avoided, may cause some to err concerning "the faith," that is, the revealed body of truth of God's Word. They miss the will of God. For the believer, the steward of God, this could result in loss at the Bema Seat. And we should note that a good steward is not only caring for treasure, he is caring for truth also.

Understanding this once again brings to my mind the importance of one's relationship with their pastor. God gave us pastors to help us grow to spiritual maturity and to watch for our souls. We must let them in! Do not lock them out!

CHAPTER 9

A BIBLICAL EXAMPLE OF
STRATEGIC PARTNERSHIP

THE APOSTLE PAUL AND THE CHURCH AT PHILIPPI

I CAN THINK OF NO GREATER EXAMPLE OF a strategic partnership where financial stewardship is so prominently illustrated than that of Paul's writing to the Philippians. Here, the Apostle Paul is commending the believers in Philippi for their partnership with him as he advanced the cause of Christ in Thessalonica, ultimately establishing a new church there. The following excerpt provides some great lessons for us.

> *But I rejoiced in the Lord greatly that now at last your care for*
> *me has flourished again; though you surely did care, but you*
> *lacked opportunity. Not that I speak in regard to need, for I*

have learned in whatever state I am, to be content: I know how to be abased, and I know how to abound. Everywhere and in all things I have learned both to be full and to be hungry, both to abound and to suffer need. I can do all things through Christ who strengthens me.

Nevertheless you have done well that you shared in my distress. Now you Philippians know also that in the beginning of the gospel, when I departed from Macedonia, no church shared with me concerning giving and receiving but you only. For even in Thessalonica you sent aid once and again for my necessities. Not that I seek the gift, but I seek the fruit that abounds to your account. Indeed I have all and abound. I am full, having received from Epaphroditus the things sent from you, a sweet-smelling aroma, an acceptable sacrifice, well pleasing to God. And my God shall supply all your need according to His riches in glory by Christ Jesus. Now to our God and Father be glory forever and ever. Amen. (Philippians 4:10-20)

Any believer should draw great encouragement from the tremendous partnership lessons we can learn from this passage.

A Source of Great Joy and Encouragement

First, we see that the Philippians' participation in this partnership for ministry was a great source of joy and encouragement to Paul, the one who labored in the ministry (verse 10). Who is not encouraged to find out someone else is on their side, or in support of their work? Can you imagine the many missionaries around the world who experience this today? Paul said that he rejoiced greatly that their care for him was flourishing! The partnership was alive and growing and a blessing to all involved.

As the leader of some non-profit organizations in my life experience, I can personally attest to the joy the workers in an organization experience when the organizations receive a gift from a generous donor. That gift makes a significant statement. It says to those serving in the organization, "I am supporting the mission in which you are laboring!" That brings a great deal of joy and encouragement to many!

Mutual Benefit

Notice that Paul did not view their support selfishly. He recognized and acknowledged that he had needs, but saw the gifts that would meet those needs as having great benefit to the givers also. It would lay up treasure in heaven for them too (verses 11-17). This is truly a healthy perspective on biblical stewardship. Paul understood God's plan for saving mankind and he accepted his role in it. All believers have a role to play in God's kingdom.

Recognition of God's Process

Another great lesson for us is that Paul recognized and acknowledged that his own dependence for provision was on God; however, he also recognized that God used His people to make that provision (verses 11-13). This is still the way God is operating today. It amazes me when I consider that I am a project on which God is working, and while He does so, He allows me to be a co-laborer with Christ. I see this as a tremendous picture of God's mercy, love, and grace all working simultaneously in my life, just as He was working in and through the Philippians and Paul. What a great God we serve!

THE VIRTUOUS WORK

Paul also recognized that the support gifts for his ministry were important and that the Philippians had "done well" in meeting these needs. This partnership was a good thing as virtuous works were the result, and he commended them for their faithful part (verse 14). Paul's commendation of the Philippians was likely an encouragement to them too, just as their support was an encouragement to Paul.

A FAITHFUL PARTNER IN MINISTRY

Paul acknowledged that the Philippians gave to meet his needs on multiple occasions. This truly was a partnership. It demonstrated a divine love as they sacrificed themselves repeatedly over an extended period (verses 10 and 16). Paul understood their love by the interest and engagement in the ministry work he was doing.

An Intimate Relationship

Paul also reminded them that they were the only church having this kind of impact on his ministry by supporting it (verse 15). Is it no wonder that he opened this epistle by saying in chapter 1:3, "*I thank my God upon every remembrance of you.*" And then he went on to recognize their "fellowship in the gospel," literally "partnering," "*always in every prayer of mine making request for you all with joy, for your fellowship in the gospel from the first day until now* (Philippians 1:4-5)." This concept is further developed in Hebrews 13:16 when the writer said, "*But do not forget to do good and to share* (literally "partner up"), *for with such sacrifices God is well pleased.*"

A Blessing to the Lord

Paul identified the gifts from the Philippians as a blessing, not only to himself, but to the Lord (verse 18). One can only imagine the delight God must experience when He sees His servants faithfully serving! He takes note of it too. Someday He will reward these faithful stewards according to their works (of what sort they were), and that will be a blessing for the Lord.

A Reciprocal Reward

Paul articulated the reciprocal nature of the partnership in the Lord's response in verse nineteen where he said, "*And my God shall supply all your need according to His riches in glory by Christ*

Jesus." In other words, because the Philippians allowed God to use them to meet Paul's needs as he ministered in Thessalonica, God would meet all their needs in similar fashion according to His riches in glory by Christ Jesus. What a promise! What a generous and thoughtful God we serve!

A Glorified God

And finally, God would receive glory from the partnership and the impact it would have on the world. This is God's purpose for man—bringing glory to Him.

CHAPTER 10

BENEFITING FROM YOUR PASTORAL RELATIONSHIP

HE WANTS TO KNOW!

IN THE FOURTH CHAPTER OF PAUL'S LETTER TO the church at Ephesus, he explains that God provides trained and gifted people to help mature the saints of God, equipping them for service. Later in the chapter, he lays out the process of "re-creating" the believer in righteousness and true holiness, or separateness from sin. When a person gets saved, there is a great need for radical change. They need to remove some old behaviors that were against the ways of God, get their attitude and understanding renovated, and then begin practicing the new ways they learn from God. God has chosen to use pastors to accomplish some of this work in our lives.

Have you ever considered that your relationship with your pastor is to be one of preparation? Your pastor should be helping "prepare" you as a believer for the Judgment Seat of Christ. In order for him to accomplish this, there are areas of your life where he will likely show particular interest. Be transparent and honest as he probes the depths of your life and soul.

SALVATION EXPERIENCE

First, your pastor wants to be sure you will be at that judgment. It is a judgment only for the saved! It is not a judgment to determine innocence or guilt, or to judge your sin. Your sin was nailed to the cross. Your pastor should want to hear your testimony of salvation directly from you. This is vital for him to hear so that he knows how to minister to your spiritual needs. If he has doubts about your salvation, that will likely limit the scope of his ministry to presentations of the Gospel and praying that you will one day believe and be saved.

Most people want to go to Heaven when they die, and many would say they are going to be there. But often, their confidence is based on a false premise. Some think keeping the Ten Commandments will get them there; however keeping them all, all the time, never happens!

Others are trusting in doing virtuous deeds or good works to earn their spot in heaven. Those will not suffice either. Being religious or being generous is not the requirement, yet this is the formula proposed by many false teachers who are delighted to be the benefactor of those good deeds or works, even money. If one's thinking and trust are not corrected, they are in danger of missing Heaven altogether.

There are not as some would say, "many paths" to Heaven. There is one, and only one! Jesus made it perfectly clear when He met with His disciples for the last supper. The Bible says, *"Jesus said to him, 'I am the way, the truth, and the life. No one comes to the Father except through Me'* (John 14:6)." No one but by him! No exceptions to this rule!

The Apostle Paul confirmed this teaching as he wrote to Pastor Timothy:

> *Therefore I exhort first of all that supplications, prayers, intercessions, and giving of thanks be made for all men, for kings and all who are in authority, that we may lead a quiet and peaceable life in all godliness and reverence. For this is good and acceptable in the sight of God our Savior, who desires all men to be saved and to come to the knowledge of the truth. <u>For there is one God and one Mediator between God and men, the Man Christ Jesus,</u> who gave Himself a ransom for all, to be testified in due time, for which I was appointed a preacher and an apostle—I am speaking the truth in Christ and not lying—a teacher of the Gentiles in faith and truth.* (1 Timothy 2:1-6)

There is only one person that can reconcile any sinner to God the Father. That person is Jesus Christ. He is the acceptable sacrifice required by the Father. He was born of a virgin, lived a sinless life, died a cruel death, shedding his blood for the remission of sins, was buried, and rose from the dead. He paid the wages of sin, which is death. He conquered death with His resurrection, and so He can offer us life—everlasting life. It is not a religion, or a series of virtuous deeds, or giving something in exchange for a ticket to Heaven. It is a person! So, that begs the question, "To what are you trusting the saving of your soul?" Or should we ask, *"Whom are you trusting?"*

The Apostle Paul takes us a little deeper into understanding this as he addresses the elders at Ephesus:

> *And when they had come to him, he said to them: "You know, from the first day that I came to Asia, in what manner I always lived among you, serving the Lord with all humility, with many tears and trials which happened to me by the plotting of the Jews; how I kept back nothing that was helpful, but proclaimed it to you, and taught you publicly and from house to house, testifying to Jews, and also to Greeks, <u>repentance toward God and faith toward our Lord Jesus Christ.</u>"* (Acts 20:18-21)

Notice a couple of very important issues in this passage. The first is that a person's repentance is toward God the Father. He is the One we have sinned against. A person with genuine sorrow turns from their sinful ways to the Father, desiring and seeking His forgiveness and reconciliation. This is what repentance looks like!

And then, by taking God at His Word, the sinner trusts the keeping of his soul to God by placing his faith in the finished work of Jesus Christ for salvation. One accepts that Jesus' sacrifice was sufficient to pay the sin debt they owed. He personalizes the reconciliation by calling upon the Lord to be his Savior. Jesus took his place, paying the death penalty on his behalf, and now in repentance, the sinner embraces the Savior.

This issue will be foremost in the mind of your pastor.

SANCTIFICATION

Once a pastor is comfortable with the testimony of the believer, he can focus his ministry on helping that believer grow in the grace and knowledge of the Lord Jesus. The Christ follower grows from being a "babe in Christ" to becoming a "mature disciple of Jesus" and an active participant in the church that Jesus is building. This is a process that continues throughout one's lifetime. It is called sanctification. The pastor exhorts and encourages the believer in their personal walk with God, the exercising of their God-given gifts and talents, their service for the Lord, and the stewardship of the resources God entrusts to them.

Then, at the end of their life on earth, they stand before the Judgment Seat of Christ. This is the judgment for the believer. The fiery judgment will be applied to a lifetime of service and stewardship. Only what was done in the will of God, with the right spirit, will stand the test and come forth as gold, silver, and precious stones. Everything else will be loss.

CHAPTER 11

EXHORTATION

IT WOULD SERVE YOU WELL TO CONTEMPLATE WHAT you have learned, or have been reminded of, in this little book as you look toward your future. Not just your future in this present life, but also your future with the Lord as you contemplate the Judgment Seat, look toward the eternity to come, and live out your everlasting life. Here are some questions you may want to consider as you muse on what you have read:

1. First and foremost, am I sure that I am saved?
2. What is my attitude about wealth today? In whom, or what, do I have my confidence?
3. How am I using the wealth God has entrusted to me? What is my activity or use of it? What am I accomplishing with my wealth?

4. Am I living with an eternal perspective, or with a temporal perspective? What do I do on purpose to maintain that perspective?

5. What strategic ministry partnerships have I formed intentionally?

6. Am I resisting the voices of opposition and avoiding being turned aside from God and His truth?

IN CONCLUSION

Let me end with this exhortation. Do not shrink away from the wonderful privilege and opportunity the Lord has afforded you in managing some of His riches. He wants you to use them to accomplish part of His plan. He wants you to experience the joy and delight of faithful stewardship and generous giving. Recognize where your wealth came from. Acknowledge to Him that you are aware of His grace toward you in this matter. Ask Him to guide and direct you in your exercise of stewardship and philanthropy. Be diligent, discerning, and generous. Experience the joy of drawing back your empty hands, and experience the wonder when He fills them up again. Then start looking for the opportunity He has in your pathway today! May God bless you, and may your reward be full.

Thank you for taking the time to read this little exhortation. I know it can be life changing and result in great blessings. I have experienced the blessings of practicing biblical stewardship for decades now. I am still learning and growing in this area of life and hope to continue until the Lord calls me home, to be with Him forever.

About The Author

DR. MIKE DUFFY and his wife of fifty-six years have three children together, as well as twelve grandchildren and four great-grandchildren. Mike's life experience is characterized by service, integrity, leadership, and accomplishment. He grew up in a home that was shattered by alcoholism when he was in elementary school. Overcoming this tragedy and trauma early in life, he has experienced productivity and success on many levels.

Mike is a combat veteran who served a tour in Vietnam with an infantry battalion of the United States Army's Eighty-Second Airborne Division. He learned early the value and reward of working hard and excelled in a corporate career for fourteen years in administrative management and sales, receiving international awards at each level for outstanding achievement and accomplishment.

Dr. Duffy received Jesus Christ as his personal Savior at age thirty-one and committed his life to Christian ministry at age thirty-five, ministering God's Word in nearly one thousand ministries nationally and internationally.

He has authored other books based on his life experience including *The Tragedies and Triumphs in an Alcoholic's Family*, *Grandpa Saw the Light*, *It's Not Too Late—A Framework to Restore a Troubled Marriage*, *It's the Cities, Stupid!*, and *The Vivid Colors of the Wounds of War*.

The following statement from Mike reveals his heart: "There is trauma and tragedy everywhere. I believe that everyone will face some adversity in life. How one responds to that adversity will shape their future. People can be paralyzed, damaged, or destroyed when adversity comes, or they can use adversity as motivation for positive change. We cannot change the past, but we do not have to live there either. We must learn from the past, look toward the future, but live today. Although no one can go back and change their beginning, they can begin today to change their ending. This is what hope looks like. I love serving God and others and have found that this approach in life is the pathway to happiness."

Endnotes

1. "Didōmi," Blue Letter Bible, accessed August 1, 2024, https://www.blueletterbible.org/lexicon/g1325/kjv/tr/0-1/.

2. "Parangellō," Blue Letter Bible, accessed August 1, 2024, https://www.blueletterbible.org/lexicon/g3853/kjv/tr/0-1/.

3. "Pronoeō," Blue Letter Bible, accessed August 1, 2024, https://www.blueletterbible.org/lexicon/g4306/kjv/tr/0-1/.

4. "Maḥăšāḇâ," Blue Letter Bible, accessed August 1, 2024, https://www.blueletterbible.org/lexicon/h4284/kjv/wlc/0-1/.

5. Steve Perry, *Living With Wealth Without Losing Your Soul: A Pastor's Journey from Guilt to Grace*, New York: RosettaBooks, 2016, 43.

6. "Lāvâ," Blue Letter Bible, accessed August 1, 2024, https://www.blueletterbible.org/lexicon/h3867/kjv/wlc/0-1/.

7. "Koinōnikos," Blue Letter Bible, accessed August 1, 2024, https://www.blueletterbible.org/lexicon/g2843/kjv/tr/0-1/.

8. Kevin Halloran, "Jim Elliot's Journal Entry with 'He is No Fool…' Quote " Kevin Halloran, accessed August 1, 2024, https://www.kevinhalloran.net/jim-elliot-quote-he-is-no-fool/.